DREAMING
FOR TWO

DREAMING
❧ FOR TWO ❧

*The Hidden Emotional Life
of Expectant Mothers*

**Sindy Greenberg, Elyse Kroll,
and Hillary Grill, M.S.W.**

DUTTON

DUTTON
Published by the Penguin Group
Penguin Putnam Inc., 375 Hudson Street, New York, New York 10014, U.S.A.
Penguin Books Ltd, 80 Strand, London WC2R 0RL, England
Penguin Books Australia Ltd, Ringwood, Victoria, Australia
Penguin Books Canada Ltd, 10 Alcorn Avenue, Toronto, Ontario, Canada M4V 3B2
Penguin Books (N.Z.) Ltd, 182–190 Wairau Road, Auckland 10, New Zealand

Penguin Books Ltd, Registered Offices: Harmondsworth, Middlesex, England

Published by Dutton, a member of Penguin Putnam Inc.

First printing, May 2002
1 3 5 7 9 10 8 6 4 2

 REGISTERED TRADEMARK—MARCA REGISTRADA

LIBRARY OF CONGRESS CATALOGING-IN-PUBLICATION DATA

Greenberg, Sindy.
  Dreaming for two : the hidden emotional life of expectant mothers / Sindy
Greenberg, Elyse Kroll, and Hillary Grill.
    p. cm.
  ISBN 0-525-94655-1 (alk. paper)
  1. Women's dreams—Case studies.   2. Pregnancy—Psychological
aspects—Case studies. I. Kroll, Elyse. II. Grill, Hillary. III. Title.

BF1099.W65 G65 2002
154.6'3'0852—dc21   2001054736

Printed in the United States of America
Set in Palatino
Designed by Eve L. Kirch

For Christopher, Chloe, and Emily

Contents

Acknowledgments   ix
Dear Reader   xi

An Introduction to Your Dreams   1

Section One—Identity

Old Self, New Self   7
Ambivalence   23
Career versus Motherhood   37
Dependency   53
Sexuality   67

Section Two—Your Relationships

Your Relationship with Your Partner   85
Your Relationship with Your Baby   99
Your Relationship with Your Family   117
Your Relationship with Your Friends and Colleagues   151

Section Three—Fears

Fears about Labor and Delivery   163
Fears about Your Baby's Health and Survival   175
Fears about Not Being a Good Mother   187
Fears about Loss of Freedom   199

Epilogue   205

Acknowledgments

This book would have been impossible to write without the participation of the women who so generously shared their dreams and experiences with us. Their contributions were invaluable in bringing our book to life and we cannot thank them enough.

There are many individuals and organizations who helped us connect with our participants by welcoming us into their classrooms and otherwise spreading the word about our project. We thank Barbara Schofield and the teachers at The Elizabeth Seton Childbearing Center; Elizabeth Bing, cofounder of Lamaze International; Michele Reinbach, a childbirth educator for the Soho Pediatric Group and St. Vincent's Hospital; Liz Schaider-Cohen of the 92nd Street Y; Marcia Westmoreland of Northside Hospital's Women First program; Bonnie Shapiro of Saint Barnabas Hospital; and all the obstetricians who posted our flyer in their offices.

We thank our agent, Harvey Klinger, for believing in our idea when it was just a twinkle in our eyes; our editors,

Trena Keating and Sara Bixler, for adopting *Dreaming for Two* and raising it as their own; Dr. Jonathan Lanzkowsky for his matchmaking skills; and Nancy Rose, Mark Frey, Susan Lafer, Darryl Patterson, Jason Anthony, Martha Cid, and Amanda Vine for lending their help and expertise.

Most of all, we thank our friends and family, especially Michael Cumella, Ethan Goldman, and Herb Sternlicht. Without their encouragement, help, patience, and general willingness to pick up the slack at home, we never could have completed this book.

Dear Reader

We wanted to take the time to explain how this book came to be. Although we fostered it along, from the moment the idea was conceived to its ultimate birth as a book, *Dreaming for Two* always possessed its own unique life.

Dreaming for Two was born of an expectant mother's dream. One night, late in her third trimester, Elyse dreamt her child was born an unruly beast, a man-child with the gaping jaws of a wild animal. The dream disturbed and frightened her, but at the same time she found herself amused. Pregnancy had certainly spruced up her dream life. Her visions during her sleeping hours had become extremely cinematic, in vivid Technicolor and rich with bizarre imagery.

Elyse confided this to her closest friends, several of whom were expectant mothers. They, in turn, confessed that the intensity of their dream lives had also increased dramatically. The discussions that followed touched on the possible meanings of these dreams, and Elyse thought the subject would make an interesting book. She mentioned the idea to her friend Sindy.

As a journalist, and having recently become engaged, Sindy was fascinated by the idea that pregnant women—with all the physiological, emotional, and psychological changes happening to them—would dream intensely. She looked to see if other books had been written on the subject and was surprised to find that while there were plenty of books explaining the physical changes women go through during their expectant months, there was not a single title that dealt comprehensively with the psychological and emotional ramifications of pregnancy. The paucity of material on the subject and our belief in its importance compelled us to move forward together with the project.

Our first step was to verify with a specialist that our idea was valid. Elyse told her obstetrician about her idea for a book on the dream life of expectant mothers, and he directed us to Hillary Grill, a psychotherapist specializing in women's reproductive health. Hillary not only confirmed that there's fertile activity taking place in a woman's unconscious during pregnancy, but she was also immediately interested in working with us on the project. Between her years of counseling expectant mothers and having had two children of her own, she'd become an expert in the complex emotional life of the pregnant woman.

With our team in place, we began speaking with pregnant women who were willing to share their dream lives with us, and found almost every person we spoke to eager and enthusiastic to share her experience. Their names have all been changed, but their dreams are real. For our purposes, the dreams are conduits—accessible channels to the varied and complex issues facing women during their metamorphosis into motherhood.

As you read on, you will notice that this book doesn't provide concrete resolutions to the issues you're facing.

Rather, the intention behind *Dreaming for Two* is to help you identify and voice your deepest feelings and concerns about your pregnancy and about becoming a mother. This helps you not only to increase self-awareness, but also to relieve anxiety and reduce depression at such a tumultuous stage of your life.

We hope *Dreaming for Two* reminds you that as you journey through what may be the greatest physiological and psychological changes of your life, you are free to explore and confront the fear and anxiety, as well as to celebrate the sometimes strange yet beautiful and euphoric feelings that are often most powerfully expressed through those fleeting images from the mind we call dreams.

Best wishes,

Sindy Greenberg, Elyse Kroll, and Hillary Grill, M.S.W.

An Introduction to Your Dreams

If dreams are, as Freud claimed, the royal road to the unconscious, then for expectant mothers, dreams are a high-speed expressway. If you're pregnant, your dream life has probably changed. Your dreams may have become richer, more vivid, and deeply entangled with the new life growing within you. Like dreaming, venturing into motherhood can seem like a journey to a faraway, mysterious, and sometimes frightening place. While doctors and scientists have charted the physical road we travel during pregnancy, the psychological and emotional changes that confront us on this journey are still shrouded in mystery.

Since the end of the nineteenth century, when Freud published *The Interpretation of Dreams*, psychotherapists of diverse schools of thought have acknowledged the connection between our dream lives and our conscious, emotional lives. When we sleep, our usual psychological and emotional defenses weaken, as do our inhibitions. This relaxing of the mind allows our dreams to depict a more honest version of our conflicts and of ourselves than we may be willing to acknowledge in our waking hours. But what exactly are dreams?

Dreams occur during the periods of sleep characterized by rapid eye movement, known as REM sleep, which begins about ninety minutes after falling asleep and occurs at regular intervals about four times a night. During REM sleep, the brain blocks out external stimuli (with the occasional exception of a ringing phone or alarm clock, which can find its way into a dream) and relates wildly disparate events, emotions, and images that wouldn't necessarily be associated with one another. Recalled in the light of day, these often bizarre and surreal nocturnal visions can provide access to the deepest recesses of the psyche. It's worth noting that we appear in nearly all our dreams and we almost always play the starring role.

Dreams are thought to represent an amalgam of unconscious conflicts, usually old, unresolved issues; conscious conflicts, generally current issues; and what Freud called the "day residue," events and images from the day. By allowing ourselves to review our conflicts while we sleep, we're attempting to work through and cope with the issues that trouble us. During pregnancy, this means our dream lives can help ease our transition to motherhood.

Each night we have an average of four to five dreams, one during each cycle of REM sleep. If you're expecting, it may seem like you're dreaming more frequently, but actually, you're just remembering more of your dreams. There are physical and psychological reasons for this. During pregnancy, we're often light sleepers. This can simply be the result of frequent trips to the bathroom, as well as the difficulty of finding a comfortable position in which to sleep. But it can also be caused by the new issues and concerns facing us—issues that are channeled into our dreams because we may be unable to confront them at any other time. The more our sleep is interrupted, the more likely we are to awaken during or close to an REM cycle, which makes it easier for us to remember our dreams.

Our dream lives during pregnancy can reveal the deep issues and concerns facing us. It can make us question everything about ourselves, including our suitability for motherhood. For example, a woman dreams she's with her baby at the supermarket, but when she looks for the baby in her shopping cart, she realizes she's left it somewhere else. Panicked, she begins ripping boxes of diapers off the shelves, looking for her baby in the spaces left behind them. The imagery of this dream—a lost or misplaced baby—can be read as feeling unprepared for motherhood. This is a common theme in the dreams of expectant mothers, so if you've dreamt similarly, rest assured that you have company and that you can be a good mother.

As you read the following dreams, you'll find they range from hilarious to frightening to surreal. You'll also become familiar with the idea of associating thoughts and feelings to dreams, looking for their signals, and cracking the codes they contain. Hopefully, this will encourage you to explore your own dreams with a sense of freedom and fun as you enter this dramatically new and exciting time of your life. You may also be surprised to discover that no matter how far your imagination takes you, you're not alone—even in your dreams.

SECTION ONE

IDENTITY

Pregnancy is all about becoming—you are becoming a mother as your fetus becomes a baby. In essence, two new identities are being formed. Now that you're expecting, you've undoubtedly considered how pregnancy and motherhood will alter not just your body, but every aspect of your life. Your relationships, career, independence, and sexuality are some of the most significant areas bound for transformation. The idea of these changes can be frightening, and you may even be embarrassed by some of your feelings—especially those that seem socially unacceptable, such as feelings of ambivalence about becoming a mother. What you may not yet realize is that with the changes brought on by pregnancy can come a sense of uncertainty about who you are and who you're becoming, or in other words, an identity crisis.

As you look forward to your baby's arrival and are caught up in all the preparation and excitement, it can be difficult to acknowledge or even recognize that you're experiencing an identity crisis of sorts. But it's important to remember that most of us experience this mixture of feelings during pregnancy and that there's something positive to be gained as you undergo these changes—by shaping your new identity, you're given an opportunity for growth, the likes of which are so rarely encountered.

Old Self, New Self

As you become a mother, the identity that has taken you a lifetime to form is now entirely up for revision.

When I become a mother, will I have to leave my old self and my old life behind?

The only dream I remember took place in an immense white house on a cliff near the ocean. It looked like the ones you would see in California and was several stories high. The dream started on the top floor of this massive house with me being chased down the stairs by a man and a woman. I'm not certain of their identities, but I was sure they were trying to kill me.

After running down the first flight of steps, I passed through an empty room. After the second flight, I landed in a room full of clocks. There were hundreds of them—alarm clocks, grandfather clocks, cuckoo clocks. The mix was very eclectic.

At the bottom of the stairs, I landed in an airy, modern foyer with picture windows looking out onto the ocean. I looked desperately for a hiding space, but the decorating scheme was very spare. Finally I found a small sofa, barely large enough for two, and crouched behind it. From my hid-

ing spot, I could hear the man talking to the woman in the
clock room. He said, "We can't find her. We have to go to
the airport." And the dream ended.

Caryn, 34, dentist

As you begin to embrace motherhood—possibly the biggest change you'll ever experience—you'll find the identity that has taken you a lifetime to form is now entirely up for revision. You may feel pressure to leave parts of your old self, and your old life, behind. This can be pressure you put upon yourself or pressure applied by the people close to you. No matter how excited you are about the upcoming birth of your child, the magnitude of the changes you're experiencing can cause tremendous anxiety and conflicting emotions.

The forty weeks of pregnancy are like a ticking clock. In that finite period, you have to prepare yourself in so many ways. While your waking hours may be devoted to getting ready for the rigors of labor and setting up your home to accommodate a baby, your dreams may be the only place where you're allowed the luxury of exploring how you feel about the more personal transformations you're going through—not the least of which is who you are becoming and how much of yourself you'll need to leave behind.

When Caryn became pregnant, she was planning to go to California on vacation with her husband. Canceling the trip was the first concrete change she made in her life because of her baby. While she was disappointed about not going away, what really disturbed her was the sense that giving up the trip felt like giving up a part of herself. For the first time, she began to consider what else she'd have to give up to become a mother and the enormous changes that lie ahead of her. The images in her dream—the clocks, the mysterious pursuers, the California house and its rooms—

reveal her feelings about change and entering this new phase of her life, feelings that are familiar to so many of us.

You're probably aware that your home, besides just being where you live, is a container for your life and that everything in it speaks in some way of who you are. This idea carries over into your dreams, where a house is often a symbol for the self—the top floor contains your conscious mind; the lower levels, your unconscious; and different rooms signify different aspects of your identity.

In Caryn's dream, there's a lot of activity and conflict going on in the house, just as there's a lot going on inside Caryn. The house's California style is a reminder of her canceled vacation; it represents her fear that her life and her sense of self will be radically transformed in the months ahead. The sea cliff where the house is perched describes her anxiety about the change.

There's a sense of dread throughout the dream, personified in the unknown couple pursuing Caryn. They're chasing her through the house, threatening her sense of self and even trying to kill it off. As Caryn runs down the stairs, it's as though she's attempting to run back in time, toward her old self. She passes through an empty room, which can be seen as an empty womb, and a wish to go back to a time in her life when there was no pregnancy. It also suggests her fears about the possibility of losing the baby.

On the next floor down, she finds the room full of clocks. This is where the baby makes itself known, as the ticking of the clocks is just like the reassuring sound of its heartbeat. On a darker note, ticking is also the sound of a bomb about to explode, and on some level this is what becoming a mother feels like for Caryn—an explosion of self after which nothing about her will ever be quite the same.

The airy, modern room at the bottom of the stairs conveys a sense of order that stands in stark contrast to the chaos of the clock room. This is where Caryn is finally able to see the future and feel okay about it. The picture windows overlooking the ocean give her a clear view of herself as part of nature—a creator of life. The foyer also symbolizes Caryn's unconscious, the space where she can resolve her feelings about having a baby and becoming a mother. When Caryn attempts to hide from her pursuers behind a sofa barely large enough for two, it suggests that she's begun to accept that she will soon have to make room in her life for her baby, as well as room in her psyche for her new identity as a mother.

As I travel toward motherhood, it sometimes feels like a bumpy ride.

I was in my hometown driving my car around a very hilly, curvy road. I've had the car since high school. It's a red Mustang convertible I call Scarlett. And I recognized the road. It's Cemetery Curve, a treacherous part of Route 1, not far from where I grew up. So I was driving around Cemetery Curve and the road was lined with rumble sticks—those bars in the road that keep trucks from going too fast—and each time I hit one I would fall out of the car, literally just roll out the door. Then I would get back in the car and check to make sure the baby was okay—and thank God, each time she was fine.

Maria, 31, stockbroker

As you begin to integrate the idea of yourself as a mother into your identity, you're beginning to say good-bye to the person you've been up until now. This is a prevalent theme in both Caryn's and Maria's dreams, even though the plot and imagery of Maria's dream about a car are completely different from Caryn's dream about a house. In our dreams, there's no single pattern of images that correlates to a particular emotion, just as there's no formula for the way this happens in our waking lives. Keep this in mind as you read this book—while you may share many of the issues and emotions evoked in these dreams, your own dream imagery may be quite different.

The journey in Maria's dream seems to span from the past to the future. Its setting, Maria's hometown, is an important part of her old identity, and the road she travels symbolizes her passage to her new one. Scarlett, her red Mustang, evokes the adventure, freedom, and sexiness Maria associates with her youth, and the road she travels with her baby evokes an unknown future.

The treacherous road and the rumble sticks causing her to fall out of the car describe the dangers inherent in Maria's journey. She seems undaunted, as she keeps moving toward her new self despite the obvious hazards along the way. Even falling out of the car is not a significant impediment—she simply picks herself up and continues on, treating the speed bumps like a pacing device that keeps her from reaching her destination too quickly. It's as if her unconscious mind is telling her it's okay to become this new person—just take your time getting there, and be careful not to lose yourself along the way.

Scarlett has been Maria's baby and she has lovingly cared for her over the years. Maria knows the feelings she's forming for her real-life baby will be far more complex than the ones she has for Scarlett. In this way, Scarlett recalls a simpler time for Maria and represents the continuum from then until now.

Like Caryn, Maria is beginning to accept her pregnancy and integrate motherhood into her identity through her dream. The baby in the car, besides portraying her actual baby, represents Maria's old, childlike self. She's keeping that part of herself safe inside the car. Her ride around Cemetery Curve helps her see she doesn't have to lose her old self altogether in order to make room for her new self and her baby. She's beginning to integrate parts of her past identity with her newly forming one, despite some bumps in the road.

I'm excited about my future as a mother, so why do I find myself clinging to my past?

I've had a lot of dreams with water imagery—showers, waterfalls, pools. I even dreamt I could breathe underwater. I think that was because of a movie I saw about babies breathing in amniotic fluid.

I remember one dream about diving underwater and looking for excavated ruins. It was at a resort and I was with a friend of mine from college, a guy I used to be really close with. We were relaxing in lounge chairs when, suddenly, it was imperative that we go diving. The water was an unbelievably radiant shade of blue and so clear. We descended and after swimming around a bit, we saw Roman and Greek ruins rising from the sand. I remember the dream because it was so bizarre and because I thought it was strange that my husband was nowhere to be found.

Tricia, 31, college admissions officer

As we enter a new phase of life, we tend to look back and remember the people who have been important to us. Like leafing through an old photo album or scrapbook, it's a way of taking stock of what we've done, who we are, and who we're becoming. So it's not surprising that at a time of such monumental change as pregnancy, we find ourselves consciously and unconsciously remembering all sorts of people. Thinking of them helps us remain connected to our past, and in some ways, that's where we'd feel more comfortable. Even though our vision of the past is probably romanticized and idealized to some degree, hidden there are parts of ourselves that we want to capture and take with us into the future to ensure they are not lost to us forever.

Tricia's dream is about the difficulty so many of us have during pregnancy letting go of our old selves and our old lives. She pictures herself relaxing in a vacation paradise with a male friend from her college years, free of responsibility, and her husband nowhere to be found. This doesn't simply imply a desire to be with another man, it suggests a longing to once again experience a relationship that's about two people and pleasure, instead of the responsibility of planning a family and a future. This idea is reinforced by the dream's exotic setting—the opposite of what Tricia imagines her life will be like after the baby comes.

When she's compelled to dive into the water, she remembers she's pregnant and no longer free to do exactly as she pleases. The urgency of the dive implies a need to protect her baby, describing how Tricia's beginning to feel the protective instinct that plays such a large part in motherhood. By diving into the deep water, it's as though Tricia is diving into amniotic fluid in order to connect with her baby. The dive also describes her preparing for rich new depths in her life; the water is clear and beautiful, indicating she's beginning to see herself clearly as a mother and that she's looking forward to the experience.

These positive feelings are juxtaposed with the image of

ruins, symbols of Tricia's old self. She dives toward them like an archeologist on an underwater dig, suggesting an effort to reclaim, or at least preserve, the parts of herself that might get left behind. It's as if Tricia fears becoming a mother will somehow ruin her, and she wants to do everything in her power to prevent that from happening.

Sometimes I feel as if my old self is in danger of slipping away.

I was standing on a frozen lake. I think it was in Vermont, and there was this really thin, frail girl in front of me who stepped on a weak spot in the ice and fell through. There were other people around, but because I was pregnant, they all rushed over to help me instead of her. I had to cry out, "No, no, I'm fine. Take care of her. She's in trouble."

Shawn, 32, midwife

During pregnancy, your life becomes so focused on preparing for your baby's arrival, it can feel as if you've ceased to exist as an individual and your sole purpose is to be a vessel for carrying your baby. Of course, this isn't the case. Just because you're having a child doesn't mean you're going to lose yourself altogether or no longer be who you were before. But the more we change and feel our lives changing, the more we need to be reassured we're still the same.

When Shawn became pregnant, as a midwife, she was familiar with the physical and emotional implications of childbirth, but still felt emotionally unprepared to step into the role of mother, especially since her pregnancy was unplanned. The setting of her dream—thin ice—conveys the feelings of danger, uncertainty, and loss of control surrounding pregnancy. It also suggests how water, an element necessary to create and sustain life, can just as easily cause life-threatening disasters.

In her dream, Shawn recognizes the frail girl who disappears through the ice as a stand-in for her pre-pregnant self, as though she was watching the person she's been up until now disappear and become frozen in time. It shocked her that no one seemed to care that this was happening, which made her feel helpless. As she directs the other people on the lake to the girl who fell through the ice, pregnant Shawn is telling them to rescue pre-pregnant Shawn. She knows the baby will change her life profoundly; still, she's asking the people around her to take care of the fragile parts of her and not just push her blindly along toward motherhood.

For Shawn, as for many of us, a major concern about letting go of her current identity is uncertainty about who she'll be once her baby's born. As she stands out there on the thin ice of pregnancy, she needs to know if mother and baby will glide through life effortlessly, or if they'll fall through into the freezing cold water. In this sense, the frail girl represents Shawn as a mother; since there's doubt about who that person will be, the image is frail and in need of aid.

The girl's frailty also describes Shawn's unborn baby— small and needy. Shawn's hoping for help taking care of her newborn because she's not sure she can do it on her own. Not wanting to let her baby or her old self slip away, she calls out to those around her to rescue them both.

Does becoming a mother mean I have to become *my* mother?

I had this dream many times when I was pregnant. It was about this poem by D. H. Lawrence I read when I was eighteen. The poem was about love and even at eighteen it made me scared about being a mom. Lawrence talks about women spending their whole lives becoming desirable, or at least trying to. He describes how they do things, how they have hobbies and interests, and how these activities make them fascinating, desirable souls. Then you get to that place—you get a mate, you have a child, and the fragmentation begins to occur.

When I started having this dream, I saw myself fragmenting. I had achieved professional success and was about to marry a famous musician who loved me very much. But in my dreams, when I watched my life, all I saw were some pieces of me—my head, my hands—floating to my husband, and other pieces—my heart, my arms—floating to my child. There wasn't enough of me left to get up and make the world a better place. It made me feel like I was going to become a hausfrau in pajamas. I didn't want to turn into this little entity that wasn't viable in the world. I didn't want my husband to think of me only as a servant for him and the baby.

That was my recurring dream, and yet it's an everyday part of my consciousness. It reminds me of when I was thirteen, watching my mother in a housedress taking care of four children. Even then I wondered if she was happy. Now I recognize and respect how much she gave us. But she gave to a point where she was empty and I don't want that to happen to me.

Charlotte, 43, singer

Throughout your life, there have probably been many people you've looked to as role models as you've shaped your sense of who you are and who you'd like to be. They may include your best friend from childhood, a favorite teacher, an aunt with a fascinating hobby, a glamorous family friend, a career mentor, or any of a number of people in your life.

Now that you're pregnant, you may find yourself looking

for an entirely new set of role models—women who have successfully integrated motherhood into their lives. You may find them among your friends, colleagues, relatives, or even people in the public eye. This process can be very subtle; you may not realize you're looking, but your antennae are up, especially if this will be your first child. But no matter how strong an influence these role models may be, when it comes to mothering, their influence cannot compare to that of one particular person—your own mother.

As we imagine ourselves as mothers, it's only natural to reflect upon who our own mother has been to us. We may conjure up images of her we react against and promise ourselves we'll never become, or we may think of her as an icon of perfection we fear we'll never achieve. Chances are, your perception of your mother falls somewhere between these two extremes, but whatever the case, that perception is essential in determining who you'll be as a parent.

This universal issue is played out in Charlotte's dream. Her sense of identity is shaken as she imagines that once she's caring for both her husband and her child, she'll be nothing but a slave to others' needs, as she perceives her own mother to have been. For Charlotte, the prospect of emulating her mother is a double-edged sword. She appreciates her mother's selflessness but fears that by following in her footsteps, she'll end up being defined solely by her role as a caretaker, and the identity she's taken a lifetime to form will disintegrate.

I worry that pregnancy and motherhood will make me unrecognizable.

I dreamt my husband and I went to Arizona to pay a surprise visit to my karate master and his wife. I used to study martial arts, and he was a very important person in my life for many years. When we entered their studio, they had no idea who we were.

While we were there, a strange, older woman came in. Her face was covered with big, brown growths that were like moles, but really huge. One was sticking out of the middle of her forehead. She claimed to be visiting the karate master for treatments. He's a hypnotherapist, and he practices a lot of alternative medicine. Since he had no idea who we were, he was very dismissive of us and left to go off with her. We felt really bad because we had come all that way to see him. I was convinced he didn't recognize me because I was pregnant.

The situation was so bizarre and tense that we decided to leave right away. As we walked out the door, a man came rushing out, but it wasn't my karate master. He's short and French with a very thick accent; this person was a tall, lanky American guy. He said, "Did you send us this post-card? We've been trying to figure out who this postcard is from." He went on to explain that they were all losing their memories, but they didn't realize it until they received our postcard in the mail. When they couldn't remember who it was from, they discovered there was some kind of environ-mental crisis going on in the town that was making people lose their memories. Apparently that was also causing the growths on this woman.

Margo, 33, chiropractor

Part of the difficulty in adjusting to your new identity as a mother is that, during pregnancy, the changes in your body are so rapid and dramatic that some days when you look in the mirror, you may hardly recognize yourself. In our image-obsessed society, where people often believe you are what you look like, you may worry that others will forget the qualities they appreciated about you before, and only notice your belly announcing that you're expecting. And you may wonder whether you'll ever look or feel like your old self again.

Margo wasn't yet comfortable with the idea of herself as a pregnant woman, let alone as a mother, when she dreamt about visiting her karate instructor. Her visit is an attempt to gauge how much of her old self she's already shed in order to become a mother. When her karate instructor, once an important role model to Margo, fails to recognize her, her disappointment expresses her difficulty letting go of her old life and her old body so she can have a child.

Margo journeys to an important place from her past to confirm she's still the same. When that doesn't happen, her dream becomes a form of denial. Even though she's consciously aware she's changing physically and that she's adapting her life for a baby, she's not quite ready to accept this, so she projects all these changes onto to those around her. Her short, French karate instructor has morphed into a lanky American, but it's really Margo's body that's changed. She attributes his forgetfulness to an environmental crisis, when the real crisis facing Margo is one of her own identity. The woman with the growths echoes Margo's sense that her body feels foreign to her, and the treatment the woman receives suggests, on some level, Margo wants her body—and her sense of identity—to return to normal.

Sometimes I'm in awe of my new, pregnant self.

You know when you study the sea world and you see the layers of hierarchies of fish, with minnows at the top and these huge whales at the bottom? When I was pregnant, in my dreams I could see all of them in full detail. I don't know if the colors were anatomically correct, but they were gorgeous. I saw a school of sea horses swimming by a coral reef that actually appeared to be breathing, and brilliant tangerine-dusted stingrays hovering in the rocks. There was a pack of minnows rendered in such a pure shade of white, they seemed translucent. I felt like part of them. I couldn't see myself swimming among them, but I know I was there. I can recall the sense of myself blissfully moving through the water. I don't think I was any particular species of fish, and I don't mean this in an earth-mother kind of way, but I can barely put into words what it felt like to believe for a moment that I belonged to this whole subterranean world of nature.

Danielle, 29, librarian

Danielle's journey though the sea world is an apt metaphor for the mix of awe and uncertainty many of us experience when contemplating ourselves as mothers. She's exploring not only being a different person, but also having a profound new connection to nature. By immersing herself in the sea world, Danielle is reveling in her own power of creation and experiencing the potency of her changing self. The water imagery here symbolizes life, and the hierarchies of fish, the stages of her baby's development. Her swim through the hierarchies is a metaphor for her own evolution toward motherhood.

Danielle imagines pregnancy as the beginning of a positive new life, filled with optimism and the sense of being part of something larger than herself—the ongoing cycle of nature. At the same time, she's uncertain about where she belongs; she knows she's part of this subterranean world, but cannot picture herself among the brilliantly colored fish. On some level, Danielle feels once she becomes a mother, she will have changed so much it will seem as if she's entered a whole other world and become an entirely new kind of being.

Like Tricia's dive toward ancient ruins, Danielle's swim through the sea world describes the bond she's beginning to develop with her baby, an experience she perceives as vibrant and beautiful. For Danielle, becoming a mother is not the end of her old self but the beginning of an exciting new part of her life she's eager to explore.

Ambivalence

Just because you're happy to be pregnant doesn't mean you're completely comfortable with the idea of being a mother.

Is it normal to want and not want a baby at the same time?

I had a nightmare that our house was hit by a tornado. I was standing in the middle of the living room holding our three-month-old son, and without warning, the picture window was sucked out by the tornado. Then a gust of wind came and snatched my baby right out of my arms and out the hole that was left where the window had been. As soon as that happened, the storm ended, leaving the rest of our home intact.

Jamie, 30, illustrator

During pregnancy, a woman is expected to feel unequivocal joy at the prospect of becoming a mother. Scratch the surface of her psyche, however, and a far more complex set of reactions will emerge. We have been biologically, culturally, and psychologically primed for motherhood. It's what we're supposed to do, free of internal conflict. But you may find yourself wondering from time to time whether all the sacrifice and change involved in becoming a mother is worth it, or if having a baby is what you really want to do. At this point, the issue is probably not whether you will or will not have the baby; you're simply acknowledging that just because you're pregnant doesn't mean you're completely comfortable with the idea of becoming a mother. In other words, you're feeling ambivalent.

Ambivalence, the simultaneous experience of both positive and negative feelings, is among the most common and least discussed sentiments experienced by expectant mothers. Even though our social mores say women should be unambiguously happy about the prospect of having a baby, it's normal to want and not want a baby at the same time. An honest depiction of an expectant mother's emotional landscape involves acknowledging that despite the numerous rewards of parenting, having a child transforms her life, and she's going to experience complex reactions to that transformation.

Pregnancy, childbirth, and adjusting to the demands of a newborn come upon us like successive storms, each with the power to churn up emotions that may have been dormant or nonexistent. Just the anticipation of these storms can be a source of tremendous anxiety. Jamie's nightmare about a tornado describes the kinds of anxieties triggered by not knowing what life will be like when you become a mother, even if it's what you've always intended to do.

There was never a question in Jamie's mind about becoming a mother. Long before she became pregnant, as early as art school, she began planning a life for herself she believed would easily accommodate a baby, even choosing a career that would be conducive to working at home. But once she became pregnant, for the first time she found herself questioning whether or not she even wanted to be a mother—a thought she felt was completely unacceptable.

For Jamie, as for most pregnant women, ambivalence about becoming a mother is so socially and psychologically unacceptable that, even in her dreams, she cannot picture herself willingly giving up her baby. Instead, she deflects the responsibility away from herself onto an outside force—a tornado.

The dream begins in Jamie's home, a representation of herself, as well as a setting that implies safety, security, and normalcy. Her house represents her life before the baby—the calm before the storm. The tornado, on the other hand, is an uncontrollable force of nature. Like the child growing in her belly, it has the power to come into her home and turn it upside down, and it does. After the tornado snatches the child from her arms and from her home, the storm ends and calm returns. The turmoil is resolved by the absence of the baby, the actual agent of change, and Jamie is left intact.

The dream describes how difficult it can be adjusting to the reality of motherhood. The swirling winds of the tornado are akin to the turmoil in Jamie's psyche. Part of Jamie is ready to embrace mothering; another part wishes the pregnancy was gone and questions her ability to care for her baby and protect him from life's many storms.

In trying to make sense of this jumble of emotions, in her dream Jamie samples life with and without her baby. By the end, she still hasn't decided what she really wants—the calm of the status quo or the storm of unknowns in motherhood.

Even though I'm pregnant, I still can't get used to the idea that I'm actually having a baby.

This is the only dream I remember since becoming pregnant. My husband and I were in our apartment, and even though the baby had been born a couple of weeks earlier, we hadn't even picked her up yet. I looked over at the computer screen and we spotted her picture online. She was wrapped in a blanket waving her arms and just generally looking really cute. We watched her for a while from the couch and cooed at the screen. Finally, I said to my husband, "Do you think we should go and pick her up?"

Sara, 31, publicist

On some level, we'd all like to have a virtual baby like the one described by Sara. This baby doesn't make any demands—there's no muss and fuss, no responsibilities, no diapers, no nighttime feedings, no need to make significant changes in oneself in order to become a mother. The baby is cordoned off at a safe distance inside a computer monitor, leaving Sara and her husband free either to proudly watch their child when the mood strikes or to push the power-off button and go out to dinner without worrying about pesky details like finding a baby-sitter. They have a baby but maintain their control, freedom, and the ability to focus solely on each other.

The only thing Sara can't do with her virtual baby is pick it up, or in other words, mother it. Her inability to hold and nurture her child in the dream is an expression of her ambivalence. It allows her to momentarily sidestep her fear and anxiety around bonding with her baby and being a good mother. For Sara, like many of us, the concept that pregnancy has a built-in deadline, ready or not, is scary.

Once you become pregnant, it can take a while to get used to the idea that the result will be a real baby. An important function of dreams during pregnancy is to help you begin actualizing your baby in your mind. When Sara had this dream, she was coming to terms with the reality of having a child. When she realizes she should go and pick up her baby, she's a step closer to embracing motherhood.

When I think of the implications of pregnancy, sometimes I want to run.

I wasn't scared about becoming a mother until I was about three months pregnant and saw a video of a fetus at my childbirth education class. That somehow induced these dreams about a serial killer. The dreams all took place in this very cold, gray warehouse with lots of stairs. In the dream, my husband and I were always running and we still had to witness all the horrible things the serial killer had done. The worst one was when the killer stabbed an infant before I could get to it.

Holly, 25, music teacher

When Holly saw the video of a fetus, she was only three months pregnant, and although she had experienced some of the less visible signs of pregnancy (like morning sickness and fatigue) she hadn't begun to show any outward signs. So in a lot of ways, her pregnancy was not real to her until she saw images of what her fetus might look like. The experience unleashed her unconscious ambivalence about becoming a mother, and even though she didn't recognize the feelings during her waking hours, it caused her to have unsettling dreams.

Expectant mothers often feel embarrassed or ashamed of the violent imagery in their dreams and can choose not to discuss them with anyone, even their partner or closest friends. But violent dreams like these are actually common during pregnancy, and they provide a useful place for working out some of our more difficult issues.

In Holly's dream, the anonymous serial killer embodies

her anxiety about motherhood. As she and her husband try to escape the killer and his crimes, they're uncertain about whether to move ahead or back—up the stairs toward the future and parenthood or down toward the past, away from it. The many stairs, all leading to danger, suggest Holly feels trapped by motherhood and sees there's no easy way out.

Even Holly's husband can't help. He's with her throughout the dream as a nod to her belief they're in this together. His presence is important to her, but that's all he really is, a presence. He plays no active role in the dream, signifying Holly's feeling that although he's there, she will ultimately be the one responsible for their baby.

The horrible things Holly and her husband are forced to witness and cannot prevent are metaphors for the awesome responsibility of raising a child. But the most disturbing image in the dream, the killer stabbing the baby before Holly could get to it, articulates her fears of her own aggressive fantasies about the baby and her ability to protect and take care of it. This imagery, like the imagery in Jamie's dream about a storm snatching her child, expresses Holly's reluctance to admit that sometimes she wishes she could make the pregnancy disappear and have her life return to the way it was before. On another level, it articulates her fear that something beyond her control could cause her to lose her pregnancy.

The killer also symbolizes Holly's ambivalence about losing a part of her current identity in order to become a mother. The cold, gray warehouse that sets the tone for the dream underscores this idea. Its function as a storage space is an expression of Holly's sense that she'll have to put parts of her life on hold while she faces the immediate challenge of raising a child.

Sometimes I'm scared that if things don't turn out the way I've imagined, I might not want this at all.

I had a dream that when my husband and I were going to the hospital to deliver the baby, my aunt was there in the lobby, waiting to greet us, dressed up like a nurse. She led us to the maternity area. I ran my hand down my stomach and it felt like it was covered in gauze, like bandages from a C-section, and I could hear all these other nurses around me blathering about how beautiful my baby was and that I had to take a look at it.

So I walked over to the nursery and looked through the window at my little girl. To me, she looked like an alien, but everyone around me kept talking about her extraordinary beauty. I panicked. Ran out of the hospital and right into my parents. Then I started to cry, "It's awful. I have a misshapen baby!" They hadn't seen her yet, and they were trying to comfort me and convince me to go back inside the hospital. But I would have none of it. I wanted to go home and be with Sam, my golden retriever.

Donna, 30, pharmacist

Pregnancy is full of unknowns that are out of our control, and it can take a while to adjust to the idea of becoming a mother and all of its mysterious implications for the future. What makes this especially difficult is that with each of these unknowns comes an idealized expectation.

Like many of us, Donna has been idealizing her delivery experience. She wants and expects it to meet the cultural ideal, in which her husband holds her hand as she pushes until a flawless cherub emerges, who, after a quick spank from the doctor, lets out a life-affirming cry.

In her dream, the presence of her aunt in the hospital lobby represents Donna's need for signs of familiarity and comfort during the unfamiliar process of labor and delivery. Donna is ambivalent about putting her body at the mercy of both her doctor and her baby. The bandages, indicating her child had been delivered surgically through a C-section, express Donna's fear that motherhood could leave her physically scarred. Since the doctor performed the C-section without her knowledge or consent, the bandages also represent the possible consequences of pregnancy she has no control over.

Another cultural ideal questioned in Donna's dream is the immediate bond that's supposed to exist between mother and baby. Donna fears this won't happen right away, if ever, which is indicated by her response to the nurses' complimentary descriptions of her baby. They think the baby is beautiful, yet Donna perceives the child as so foreign, it might as well be from another planet. Her reaction describes her fear that not only will she be incapable of bonding, but that she may not even like her baby. She also wonders if something's wrong with her for not recognizing the beauty that's so obvious to everyone else.

Donna's flight from her little alien baby expresses her ambivalence; she runs but is conflicted about whether or not it's the appropriate reaction. When she flees the hospital and meets her parents, it's as though she's confronting her conscience. Her parents encourage her to go back and own up to her responsibility for her baby, but Donna wants none of it. She's overwhelmed by the sheer magnitude of motherhood and wishes only to go back to her dog and the comfort of what's familiar.

Even though I'm looking forward to motherhood, I worry it will be an obstacle in my life.

When I became pregnant I dreamt I was walking home from class or a job. It was a fairly long walk, a couple of miles or so, and I thought I knew the way. At one point I came to a turn and thought, "Oh, I'll turn here because it's a scenic route, and there will be more interesting things to look at."

As I continued to walk, the sky grew dark, and I entered not such a great part of town. For safety reasons, I decided instead of being on the street, I'd cut through a building, which was some sort of institution or school. But instead of cutting through, after entering the building, I got on a glass elevator.

Normally I'm not afraid of heights, but there were lots and lots of people on this elevator, and my face was pushed up against the glass as it shot up two hundred floors. It was so horrible watching the scene below while we were moving so quickly. When I got off the elevator I thought, "Oh, God, now I have to go down two hundred flights," and decided to walk.

After descending fifty flights of stairs I came across a human car wash exhibit, which involved participation. Big, round, bristly brushes washed my entire body; then an industrial dryer came over my head. When it was over, I wasn't really dry, and I was annoyed that I had to walk down 150 more flights of stairs while still damp. I don't know if I ever got home in this dream. I think more and more things kept happening to keep me from what I should be doing.

Anne, 28, graduate student

When Anne became pregnant she was unmarried, in school, and not planning to have a child. While she loved her boyfriend (now her husband) and he wanted to have a

baby, at the time she learned she was pregnant, she was focused on becoming a therapist. As for many of us, a major
source of Anne's ambivalence about having a baby is the
idea that it may prevent her from reaching her goals, professional and otherwise. In her dream, Anne is like Dorothy
trying to get back to Kansas, but without a pair of ruby slip-
pers to help her. The endless, obstacle-ridden journey symbolizes her fear that pregnancy is preventing her from
moving ahead with her own life, and her ambivalence is expressed by never getting where she wants to go.

Anne's walk home can be seen as the journey of pregnancy with motherhood as the destination. Her choice to
take the scenic route portrays Anne's positive feelings
about being pregnant and becoming a mother—the part
that delights in the idea of parenting and the powerful feelings associated with the act of creation. The journey's turn
for the ominous mirrors her anxiety about motherhood.

When Anne enters the building in an attempt to find
safety, but finds herself on a fast-moving elevator, it suggests both a wish to maintain the psychological safety of
her life before pregnancy and her fear of the fast-paced
changes happening to her. In the elevator, her face is
pushed up against the glass, an image that says she's feeling trapped in her new role; she sees her old life ebb into the
distance as she hurtles toward her next phase.

The two hundred flights up-and-down describe Anne's
ambivalence. Like Holly in the warehouse, Anne is unsure if
she should go up toward motherhood or race down toward
her old life. She knows if she continues upward, she'll even-
tually reach motherhood, but as she approaches her new role,
she panics and decides to walk down, back to her old self.

After descending just fifty flights, Anne is faced with the
obstacle of the human car wash, a metaphor for labor and

delivery, which makes her realize that becoming a mother is inevitable. She's annoyed that she still faces so many flights down while uncomfortably damp, just as in her waking life she's troubled by the idea that her journey to motherhood will include some discomfort, and that it will not end with delivery.

I'm afraid I won't be up to the task of mothering—physically or emotionally.

I'm eight months pregnant, and a few days ago I dreamt about a baby girl, even though I know I'm having a boy. She could stand in my arms, so she must have been about a year old. And she was very cute, blond and pretty. I, on the other hand, was loaded with stuff—bags, carriage, toys. I couldn't escape the feeling of being overloaded. Every time I put something down, another toy or baby bottle would appear in my arms. I was happy to be with the baby, but I was positive I would soon collapse.

Katherine, 28, photographer

When Katherine had this dream, she was in her eighth month and quite familiar with the sensation of feeling physically overloaded. The slapstick juggling act she performs in her dream with all the baby equipment suggests she's feeling not only physically burdened by pregnancy, but emotionally overwhelmed by it as well. Katherine's looking forward to being a mother, and in her dream, she pictures herself happy to be with her beautiful baby. But her confusion about what she really wants is expressed by her imagining she has a girl when she knows she's really having a boy. On some level, Katherine wishes she could once again be a beautiful child like the one in her arms, free of the responsibilities and changes she's about to face. On another, she longs for reassurance that she'll be able to cope with the burdens of motherhood.

After months of morning sickness and gaining weight, becoming a swinger sounds much more appealing than becoming a mother.

I dreamt my husband and I were in this posh bachelor pad which was very sleek and elegant, but cold. The only thing I really liked there was this big tank filled with brilliantly colored exotic fish and plant life. It was an informal gathering of couples—some were close friends, others not so close.

Early in the night the idea surfaced that we should have a partner swap. We scheduled the event for 10:50 P.M. At that time, the women would gather with makeup and hair accessories to primp. Then at 1:00 A.M. we would join the fellows at the party and mingle. I remember having mixed feelings and being uncomfortable with not knowing who either my or my husband's partner would be. I did, however, feel confident in my body. I was post-baby and not shy. I knew my body would be admired.

Yvette, 41, insurance agent

Who wouldn't prefer a night of group primping, sleek apartments, and no-strings attached rendezvous to sore joints, swollen ankles, and elastic-waist pants? Yet for Yvette, after months of pregnancy, the sleek and elegant habitat of the singles crowd doesn't seem all that appealing. In fact, it seems foreign and cold. The only thing there she can relate to is the fish tank, which, like her pregnant belly, is full of liquid and life. Yvette's dream truly exemplifies ambivalence, since in every aspect she has her swollen ankles in two places: Some friends are close, others not so close; she wants to swap partners but is uncomfortable not knowing who she and her husband will end up with; she's pregnant in her waking life, but post-baby in her dream.

Despite her feelings of separateness, in her dream she sees herself as a beautiful, nonpregnant woman—an exotic fish swimming toward a sexual adventure. It's as if she had to make herself nonpregnant to feel sexual and sexually attractive, leading her to question her new identity as a pregnant woman and as a mother. To help her escape these feelings, she imagines she'll be admired, reassuring her that whatever uneasiness she's experiencing, she'll once again feel sexually attractive.

When Yvette questions who her partner will be, she's not only thinking of what another man would be like, she's also questioning her marriage's ability to withstand the addition of a child. Yvette is not swapping partners, but one self for another, bad feelings about motherhood for good ones, one day to the next. With her designated primping time, Yvette seems to be saying, "If I can just have some extra time to prepare myself, I'll be more comfortable with the idea of myself as a mother."

Career versus Motherhood

No matter what choices you've made, they will involve some compromise and challenge your sense of who you are.

When it comes to choices about career and motherhood, I feel society sends women mixed and confusing messages.

I bought the cutest little stuffed toy at the flea market—an old blue leather camel—and being due in three weeks I justified my purchase as being for the baby, even though the little camel was really for Mommy.

That night I dreamt I'd had the baby—a boy, which I already knew from my amnio. But this was no baby. He was a fully grown, lanky, and hairy eighteen-year-old, without a trace of babyish cuteness or cuddliness about him. Stranger still, he was part boy and part camel. You couldn't tell by looking at him. He wasn't on all fours and had no hump. But as his mother I instinctively knew, and when he opened his mouth and his enormous teeth started chomping, his camelness was undeniable.

I had no idea what to feed him. What does a teenage camel-boy eat anyway? Just about anything, it turns out. The only food I had was beautiful Christmas cookies shaped like the animals of Noah's Ark that looked almost too good to eat. They were arranged in tableaux all around my house, and I was preparing them for a photo shoot.

Before I knew it, Camel Boy was chomping their heads off, one by one, and within minutes, they were all decapitated. I couldn't bring myself to yell at my new baby, so I gently pleaded with him to stop, but either he didn't understand me or he chose to ignore me. I felt like a terrible mother for not having the proper food for him and for not knowing how to control him, and like a terrible employee for letting my child destroy an expensive photo shoot.

Elyse, 35, coauthor, *Dreaming for Two*

Where becoming a mother was once the gold standard of adulthood for women, building a career is now considered an equally important part of maturing. As young women, we're often made to feel that succeeding in the working world should be the most important part of our lives. By the time we're ready to have children, many of us have spent countless hours working toward that goal, and possibly a small fortune on tuition, and are proud of our accomplishments. Still, no matter what else is going on in a mother's life, it's almost a given that she'll be the primary nurturer. We're expected— and often expect ourselves—to seamlessly incorporate babies into our lives. Integrating work and motherhood can make us worry that we won't be able to perform either task well, since it always entails some kind of compromise. It's no wonder conflicting emotions about the idea of juggling a career and motherhood can precipitate an identity crisis of sorts.

For many of us, until pregnancy, our identity has been defined largely by the work we do. This self-definition can come from a passion for our work, the notion of ourself as a working person, or the satisfaction and independence that come from earning a salary. The need to support our family is also a consideration when deciding what we'll do careerwise, once the baby's born. Some women would love to stop working, or at least cut down on the amount of time spent on the job, but can't because of financial constraints. Others feel guilty about their desire to work because their reasons for working are more personal than financial. And for some women, there's no choice but to stay at home because of inadequate childcare options.

The social consequences of working—or not working—can feel like a no-win situation. By continuing to work, you may fear you'll be condemned by some as not being a committed enough mother. But if you decide to stay home with your baby, you may miss the interaction with friends and colleagues you enjoyed before, and fear losing their respect, as well as the status society confers on working people. You may also be concerned about how becoming a stay-at-home mom will affect your relationship with your partner.

Elyse's dream describes the balancing act many of us face as we try to reconcile the demands of a career with the demands of motherhood. Elyse's identity has always been closely linked with her work. Now that she's having a baby, she fears her capacity to do a good job and focus on her professional commitments is in jeopardy. This fear is embodied by the baby in her dream—he's a grown-up camel-boy whose hidden animal attributes make him unpredictable and capable of destroying things that are important to her, including parts of herself. If we understand the cookies as being aspects of her, then his action, biting off their heads, symbolizes her fear that the chaos and added responsibility of motherhood will make her lose her mind. Because the cookies are related to her job, the act also points to her fear that in becoming a mother, she may have to give up her professional self.

For those of us whose identities are strongly intertwined with our work, there can be a sense of bewilderment about how we'll apportion our time and emotions once the baby arrives. We may feel torn between personal gratification and doing what we believe to be best for the baby. In Elyse's dream, her baby is almost a full-grown man—she never gets to nurture the cute, cuddly infant she's been anticipating. This represents her concern that focusing too much on her career will cause her to miss out on her son's childhood, as well as her fear that having a baby may deprive her of her own adulthood, or at least the version of adulthood she has known.

Elyse's dream also points to her anxieties about being a nurturer, a feeling shared by many of us who have focused our energies on our careers. Whatever her accomplishments have been up to this point, she fears they'll amount to nothing in the face of the new skills she'll need to learn. In her dream, Elyse is completely unprepared for the camel-boy; his gaping jaws and gigantic teeth embody her fears about taking care of her baby, especially nursing him. Her baby's need to be fed wreaks havoc on her job, echoing the fear shared by so many of us that once our baby's born, we'll fall short at both motherhood and our career.

The prospect of developing a career and becoming a mother at the same time seems daunting.

During my pregnancy, I had several dreams about men in their forties and fifties wearing diapers over their business suits. They were all in motion, briefcases in hand, walking purposefully down the street to their offices. I just watched them from above. My bird's-eye view revealed all the telltale signs of aging—bald spots, potbellies, sagging butts. I woke myself up laughing, and I must have woken my husband, too. He looked over at me and asked, "What's going on?" But I couldn't quite bring myself to tell him. I just said, "I'll fill you in tomorrow morning."

Carolyn, 27, graduate student

For most people, their twenties and thirties is the time spent focusing on building a career. As women, we have the added challenge of this period coinciding with the years in which we'll most likely have children. Carolyn was in school when she became pregnant, and although she and her partner had discussed having a child, she wanted to start her career before plunging into motherhood. Now, although she's enjoying pregnancy and looking forward to becoming a mother, she can't help feeling like an outsider in the professional world. This is expressed in her dream by her role as an observer. As she watches the men walking purposefully to work, she wonders if she'll ever be included in that world or if she'll be always saddled with diapers. She can't imagine how she'll be able to progress in her studies or begin a career once there's a baby attached to her.

The incongruous image of grown men wearing diapers is more than just funny, it's a stand-in for Carolyn's complex feelings about motherhood. In some ways, they represent the baby being in control of her and her life's direction; the baby is walking purposefully and knows what he wants and needs, and Carolyn knows her role is to be the one to fulfill those needs. The diapered men also represent her husband and her fear that rather than being an equal partner in caring for their baby, he'll require taking care of, too.

I worry that the expense of raising a child will lower my standard of living.

I dreamt I was at the estate my cousin just bought. There's a big barn on the property, and I left my baby there alone because I had to go see a client. I hadn't even nursed it yet. Throughout the session I was anxious about getting back to the baby. But when I got back I was even more anxious about nursing. I realized I didn't know what to do. I searched furiously for a private spot, not because I was self-conscious about my body, but because there were people everywhere, and I was embarrassed that I didn't know how to nurse my child.

Sunita, 33, psychotherapist

For many young couples, the decision to have children comes just at the time when their combined salaries can afford them a comfortable lifestyle, often for the first time in their adult lives. During pregnancy, couples become aware that the expense of raising a child, along with the potential loss or decrease of an income, can significantly alter their standard of living. For a single mother, the ramifications can be even more profound.

When faced with decisions about career and motherhood, this hard reality forces many of us to question our priorities and what quality of life means to us. We may feel guilty about returning to work if its main purpose is to maintain the standard of living we've become accustomed to. Or we may worry that our baby won't know us if we spend most of its waking hours at the office. We may also wonder what we're willing to sacrifice materially to meet society's ideal of a good mother.

For the first part of Sunita's marriage, her husband was in graduate school, and they depended upon her salary to get by. Now that her husband is about to enter the professional world and she's about to become a mother, her status, both in her marriage and at work, is rapidly changing. Soon she'll no longer be her family's sole breadwinner. Plus, as a psychotherapist with a private practice, her income directly relates to the number of clients she sees. Once the baby arrives, that number will most likely decrease.

For Sunita, visiting a large estate like the one in her dream describes her feeling that becoming a mother will make attaining financial success more difficult and that she may never have all the material comforts she desires. When she arrives at the estate, she's unprepared to care for her baby and work at the same time. She perceives the baby as a hindrance and leaves it in the barn while she goes off to see a client. The barn is a metaphor for the uterus; leaving her infant alone there suggests that she wants to put the baby back inside because she isn't ready to be a mother. She has some things to figure out first, not the least of which is how she'll integrate the baby with her career and be a good mother.

The question of how to allocate your time once you become a mother is not easy. In Sunita's dream, she's constantly worrying about how she'll find time to bond with and take care of her baby and continue her career. When she's with her client, she thinks constantly about her baby; when she's with her baby, her fear that her lack of mothering skills will be exposed is so pronounced that she attempts to hide with the child. It's as if she believes that because she spends time working, she's forfeited her competence as a mother, even though her career involves taking care of people and she's comfortable in that role.

**I know how to do my job, but I'm afraid I won't
know how to be a mother.**

I had extremely vivid and scary recurring dreams during my first pregnancy. I would see myself driving down a highway through the Great Plains, being forced to look at fields littered with severed limbs, babies with animal heads, and decapitated horses and rabbits. In a lot of these dreams, I felt like I was being chased. I wanted to run and yell but was encumbered by an overwhelming sense of paralysis.

The highway led to a dusty old ghost town that I haven't thought about since I was a child. When I was little, I used to dream that a witch was chasing me through towns like this, and I would hide from her in the bottom of a castle. I don't know who is chasing me now.

Eileen, 33, attorney

For the ten years before Eileen became pregnant, she worked literally day and night to secure her position in a prominent law firm. But she became suspicious of the corporate world when after conceiving on her honeymoon, the only thing her office buddies wanted to know was how much time off she'd be taking. Eileen had more pressing concerns. Before she found out she was pregnant, she'd been drinking socially and taking antibiotics for what she thought was malaria but turned out to be morning sickness. So until she had her amnio, Eileen feared her actions might have hurt her baby. Her guilt is expressed in the horrific images she saw in the dream, where having a damaged child was not only the consequence of her behavior, but the retribution for it, too.

Eileen worked until her sixth month, the last month part-time, which in her office meant a forty-hour week. Then her doctor forced her to go on disability because of stress, much of it triggered by the prospect of handling her workload once she becomes a mother. Her sense of self has been drawn from her career as an attorney, and she hardly had time to adjust to being a wife when she became pregnant. Having a baby felt like another enormous pressure.

Eileen's fears about what motherhood might mean giving up were so strong, they made themselves known time and again in her dreams. The severed limbs and decapitated animals she encounters while driving down the highway symbolize her feeling that no matter what choices she makes in the months ahead, she'll be losing parts of herself and will feel incomplete. Like the decapitated cookies in Elyse's dream, the headless animals imply that Eileen worries about losing her mind as a mother and also worries that her intellect, so valued in her profession, has not equipped her for mothering.

The highway itself is a classic metaphor for journeying into the past and toward the future. That it leads to a ghost town, a dream image Eileen remembers from childhood, suggests this is where her pre-pregnant self resides, and the road to the future is marriage and motherhood. This journey raises fear and anxiety, as it's taking her into a new world. In her career, Eileen knew who she was and what she was striving for; the path of motherhood is less clear. Her anxieties about being a mother and the health and survival of her baby so overwhelm her that in her dream, she feels paralyzed. She wants to escape, but she can't.

The animals she encounters on this journey—rabbits and horses—possess opposing traits, representing the opposing sides of Eileen and her conflict about becoming a mother. Eileen's career makes her feel powerful, like the horse. But as a mother, she imagines she will have to become more rabbitlike—soft, vulnerable, and iconic of reproduction. The cultural connotation of having a career versus being a mom also plays into this juxtaposition of rabbit and horse. Women with careers are often perceived as strong, and their skills are valued by society. A corporate attorney, for example, can bill more than three hundred dollars an hour. A mom is viewed as just a mom; it's impossible to place monetary value on the work she does, and her skills are taken for granted as inherent, not something one has to train for. Like many of us, Eileen stores these stereotypes in her unconscious mind, even though she knows, on another level, becoming a mother will actually be an enormous challenge that will require horselike strength.

I worry that babies and pregnant bodies aren't conducive to my work environment.

I was driving down the highway with a group of people from work. We were trying to go to my brother's apartment, but we couldn't get across town because we turned too late and were caught in a flood. We were up to our shoulders in water and there was so much of it lapping around that we had to swim. I must have looked very funny, this pregnant woman swimming around the highway. Everyone around me kept asking if I was okay.

Kendall, 31, Internet producer

Before Kendall became pregnant, her life revolved around her career, her husband, and her friends and colleagues. She always knew that starting a family would alter her life's course. But as her due date approaches and her pregnant body becomes a visual announcement of her decision to have a baby, she's beginning to feel different from the people around her, and anxious about the changes the baby will bring—especially in her professional life.

Kendall sees her pregnancy as an event that's taking her down a new road, but one that also leads back to her family of origin. It's her family who shaped her idea of what it means to be a parent, with whom she feels safe, and with whom she associates her role as someone's child. When she pictures herself with a group of colleagues driving to her brother's apartment, instead of the office, it expresses her concern that this new direction of pregnancy will make her lose her professional edge and derail her career. Kendall has difficulty navigating her dual roles of working woman and expectant mother, and fears it will change her relationship with her colleagues who, when faced with the flood, perceive her as being helpless. The imagery suggests Kendall is trapped by a force outside her control, and certainly describes the way many of us feel when faced with the prospect of integrating our career with motherhood.

The flooding water can also be seen as a metaphor for amniotic fluid. Kendall worries her water will break at an inopportune time and her anxiety about this is amplified by her husband, a doctor, who has begun lining their bed and sofa with Chux, the large absorbent pads used in hospitals. All those Chux around the house have increased Kendall's anxiety about her water breaking, but she's less concerned about soaking her bed than she is about the public humiliation of causing a flood during a business meeting.

In the workplace, pregnancy broadcasts things about a woman's personal life that a nonpregnant person would never have to reveal. Your growing belly becomes a billboard announcing that you're sexually active and have cho-

sen to have a family—information that in a professional setting one might normally decline to share.

The physicality of pregnancy can feel like an encum-
brance in any scenario, but is especially pronounced in
the workplace. Interruptions for frequent doctor appoint-
ments, and even bathroom breaks, can make us feel self-
conscious that our colleagues perceive us as needing
preferential treatment. We may also worry they'll resent
us if their workloads increase as a result of our decision
to have children. In her dream, Kendall is hyperaware of
the physical difference between her and her colleagues;
during the flood she sees herself as clownish, suggesting
she sees her pregnant body and her baby as things that
will get in the way of work and alienate her from her colleagues.

Who will I be able to trust with my baby while I'm at work?

*This dream occurred after my fifth month, and I knew I
was having a boy. It involves a couple of people from my department who I used to be very friendly with—one's a guy
named Raul, and the other, a woman named Janet. They're
both in their mid-to-late twenties and were very excited
about my pregnancy.*

*In the dream, Raul and Janet were supposed to be watch-
ing my baby—a girl with a full head of brown hair. They
must have put her on the changing table, then left the room
or turned away or something, because the baby was on the
floor motionless and she had blood running out of her ear.
It was horrifying.*

*I woke up completely shaken. The only comfort I had was
that it couldn't have been my baby, since I knew I was car-*

rying a boy. I vowed to myself that I would never leave my
baby alone with either Raul or Janet.

Hope, 36, communications director

Hope's dream depicts the greatest fear many of us have about returning to work—the risk inherent in leaving our baby in someone else's care. Entrusting another person with our most precious possession—especially if that person is a stranger—along with the desire or need to resume our career, creates a conflict that, for many of us, has no perfect resolution. If we choose to return to work, we may feel guilty and anxious about how our choice will affect our baby. And if we decide to stay at home, we may fear we'll become resentful that we had to give up our career, or at least put it on hold.

Competition in the workplace and fear of either being demoted or replaced also play a strong role in Hope's dream. The baby, a girl with physical attributes similar to her own, is a stand-in for Hope, and her colleagues' disregard for her safety is a metaphor for her fear that she can't trust them to look out for her best interests while she's home on maternity leave. Unfortunately, Hope's fears were not unfounded; when she returned to work, huge reorganizations and staffing changes had occurred—Raul got her job and Janet reported to him.

Having worked throughout my adult life, I'm conflicted about the idea of being a stay-at-home mom.

I had this dream shortly after I left my job. I was very successful in real estate, but hated it. When I became pregnant, I decided to leave my job and planned to make a total career change after the baby came. So for a while, I threw

myself into being an exemplary corporate wife, and my hus-
band and I would entertain at home constantly. I think that
led to this dream.

I was cooking for a big dinner party we were hosting for
important business associates of my husband. There was a
turkey baster on the kitchen counter, which is unexcep-
tional but for the fact that it was about twice the size of a
normal turkey baster, and that I was not cooking a turkey.
I can't say why, but I instinctively knew the baster was the
enemy. It started squirting everywhere and I had to stay out
of its path because if any of its liquid was to hit me, I would
get pregnant. I was already big and pregnant, but somehow,
it could make me more pregnant than I already was.

Nan, 33, homemaker

Besides being the enemy, it doesn't take great leaps of
the imagination to see that the turkey baster represents a
phallus in this context. Nan's dream does, however, contain much more than sexual imagery. It explores her concept of what it means to be a stay-at-home mother and her
attitude toward traditional sex-role stereotypes. Her choice
to leave her successful career and devote herself to caring
for her baby suggests that when she had this dream, she
was not just adjusting to the idea of becoming a mother,
but also the loss of her role as a career person, at least for
the time being.

Like many women, Nan sees staying home with her
newborn as the perfect opportunity to plan a career change.
Still, she doesn't feel completely comfortable in her interim
role of corporate wife. She thinks it will leave her under-
stimulated and possibly make her less interesting. The
turkey baster symbolizes the male world, which she feels
has now relegated her to being a servant. And she's angry

at her husband who, as part of the male world, can make her even more of what, on some level, she doesn't want to be—a mother, especially one who's confined to the home. Nan wonders if she might be better off with a turkey baster of her own, since it seems to her that her husband's got it made. He gets to have a baby and go on with his life as usual.

Dependency

Becoming a mother makes you question who you can depend on, just as you're realizing a baby will soon be completely dependent upon you.

Now that I'm having a baby, I find myself depending on my partner in a completely new way.

During my last trimester, I had all sorts of horrible dreams about my husband dying in an accident. All of the dreams would start out the same—he would kiss me good-bye, then leave for work. Moments later, the phone would ring, and I'd learn that he'd just met some terrible fate. In one of these dreams he'd been pushed in front of a moving subway car, in another he'd been shot in a deli robbery, and in yet another, a chunk of loose concrete fell off a building and crushed his skull while he was walking below.

I probably had a dozen versions of this dream—other than the details of the accident, they were all pretty much the same. I'd get the call, hear the news and start sobbing uncontrollably, and then the dream would end. It sounds crazy, but these dreams shook me up so badly that now when he leaves the house in real life I worry it's the last time I'll ever see him.

Hannah, 36, editor

No matter how intimate your relationship with your partner was pre-pregnancy, now that he's the father of your baby, you probably find yourself depending upon him in a completely new way. The thought of losing him—and the support system he represents—can be almost unbearable. These feelings of dependency and vulnerability experienced by so many of us during pregnancy are expressed in Hannah's dream. The image of an uncontrollable force taking her husband's life articulates her anxiety about being left alone to care for her baby and her need for reassurance that this won't happen.

During pregnancy, as we start planning to care for a baby, our partner isn't the only person we begin to depend upon in a new way. We depend upon our doctor for the safe delivery of our baby, our family to be there for us in a new capacity, and a variety of caregivers. We even find ourselves depending upon a host of strangers, be it the person who offers us their seat on the bus or the storeowner who lets us use their bathroom.

Dependency issues have a lot to do with your family of origin, and the degree to which you were able to rely upon them. During pregnancy, these issues are magnified by the realization that you'll be continuing this familial cycle and that someone will be utterly dependent upon you as you were upon your parents. As a result, you may be confronting issues you never even knew you had, and issues you thought you'd learned to deal with can resurface in new ways.

Finances can also play a large role in dependency issues. Regardless of whether you plan to work or stay at home after the baby's born, your partner's income will probably take on a greater significance. Hannah, for example, realized that even if she returns to work after her maternity leave, with the increase in their household expenses, she'll need to rely upon her husband financially for the first time in their marriage. For many of us, like Hannah, who have worked throughout our adult lives, the idea that we'll now have to rely upon our partner financially can compromise our self-esteem. And the thought that losing him could mean losing the ability to support our child can be terrifying.

As relationships shift with the prospective arrival of a newborn, even though you may find the idea threatening, it's normal to reevaluate how and to what degree you're going to be able to comfortably depend upon your partner once your child is born.

Sometimes I fantasize about being taken care of completely.

There doesn't seem to be a beginning to the dream, I'm just suddenly there in it. I'm walking through the halls of a medieval castle filled with more rooms than I can imagine. I stop and open the doors to several of them to see what's going on inside. Each room contains a different workshop or project. Groups of people, mostly women, are bustling about making things—things made of flowers and lace, sewn and hot-glued together. I discover that my stepmother has arranged all these workshops to prepare for an event taking place later that day. I'm not alone. A guide is with me.

Later in the afternoon, I'm standing with hundreds of people in a field. Banners are flying and there are horses with ribbons in their manes. My father is sitting on a throne up on a hill surrounded by knights holding jousting poles in the air. Suddenly, a group of people enters on horses, one horseman standing out among the rest. He stops before my father

*and asks him for my hand in marriage. Just then I realize
everything I'd seen in the castle makes sense and I feel swept
off my feet. I also remember that I'm already married.*

Luisa, 30, industrial designer

As life becomes more complicated, we may long for an
idealized version of childhood where all our needs are met
and we're the center of our family's attention. Luisa's
dream about a magical world where she's fussed over and
taken care of like a princess in a fairy tale couldn't be further from her waking life, in which she's married, pregnant
with her second child, and running a business with her husband. It's a fantasy version of marriage seen from a childlike perspective, whereupon taking your vows you have a
husband who takes care of you completely.

While dependency issues often deal with the discomfort
of relying upon others, this dream expresses a deep desire to
depend upon others entirely. By casting herself in the role of
princess, Luisa is giving herself over to the ultimate escapist
fantasy and asking those around her to take over. The events
of the dream suggest she's feeling overwhelmed by her daily
life and hoping that if she could just give herself over to other
people, her life would be easier and more manageable.

In her dream, the castle represents Luisa, and she can
see her inner process working in its many rooms, repre-
sentations of her unconscious mind. Each character serves
a different purpose. The trustworthy guide who helps her
navigate the many rooms and workshops, themselves
symbols of her need for help and guidance, suggests Luisa
feels so overwhelmed she can't even navigate her own
mind. Her stepmother is the doer, the one who organizes,
and even tries to control her life and mind. Her father, the
king, is an über-father who arranges her marriage and runs

her life just as he runs his kingdom. The horseman is, of course, Prince Charming, the fantasy man who sweeps her off her feet and with whom she'll live happily ever after. The only glitch is that she's already married and a mother— she's made her choices, and there's a family at home depending upon her to take care of them and not escape.

Pregnancy has made me question whom I can truly depend upon.

Since I was a kid, I've always hated clowns. When I went to the circus, they scared me. I didn't think they were funny. In my dream, I'm on a stage set and this clown appears and he's trying to kill me. Then, poof! He disappears and I'm left on the set with a pile of clown clothes.

After that, the dream flashes to me lying in bed. I'm very aware of my pregnancy at this moment, cognizant of being two. There's a very nice person at my side, a man. I don't know if he's my husband or a family member or what. But as I said, he's very nice and he's holding my hand and making me feel much better.

The dream then moves to a supermarket, which I believe to be empty except for this very nice person and me. But then the nice person leaves and I see this heavyset guy strolling down the aisle. He's singing and calling out to me, "I'm going to hurt you." I soon realize this fat man is the clown. I woke in a state of sheer panic and told my husband, "Honey, I'm being attacked by a killer clown." He didn't quite get the terror of it all.

Susan, 42, marketing consultant

Clowns have always scared Susan. Even though most people consider them to be icons of laughter and fun, her attitude toward clowns has always been the opposite of what's expected. In many ways, she's experiencing a similar reaction to pregnancy.

For Susan, discovering she was pregnant felt like nothing short of a miracle. As a young woman, she had an elective abortion, and after years of being sexually active and sometimes slipping up on birth control, Susan assumed she could no longer become pregnant. Now that she's pregnant and its implications have become real, she's surprised her reactions to the prospect of becoming a mother are not limited to joy and assurance that everything will work out. Susan's pregnancy has brought with it a new and unexpected set of fears about depending upon a man to take care of her and having an infant depend upon her completely.

The dream begins on a stage set, a location that implies playing a part, with Susan acting in her new role of expectant mother. The role marks an especially dramatic change for Susan, since she married at age forty and became pregnant a year later. Not yet secure in this new role, Susan feels threatened, and she's unsure about whom she can turn to for protection and just what kind of protection she needs.

The vanishing clown is seen as a killer; he represents a terrifying idea—Susan's fear that at any moment her pregnancy, and perhaps her new life, can disappear. This image of sudden loss is fueled in part by her feelings about having had an abortion. Like many expectant mothers who at some point have chosen to terminate a pregnancy, Susan feels guilty and questions if she deserves this baby.

In her dream, Susan finds security and relief in the company of an anonymous but very nice man—a fantasy protector for herself and the baby. The anonymity of the person suggests she cannot imagine who will actually be there for her in this way once her baby arrives. Will it be her husband?

In the dream she's not sure. She just knows the desire to depend upon someone fully is unfamiliar to her and is itself a source of tremendous anxiety. Still she wants—and feels like she needs—to have a very nice person to guide and protect her through this pregnancy and the years to come. When she's with the nice man she's comfortable, but the moment he leaves, the clown reappears, and she once again feels unprotected. It's as if her unconscious is voicing her deepest fears about her partner's ability to provide for her needs and the possibility he will abandon her to care for the baby herself.

Susan's need for an escort in domestic spheres like the bedroom and the supermarket suggests she's insecure about her ability to play the role of mother to a completely dependent newborn. In this regard, the clown appearing in the supermarket as an overweight man represents the baby, and the nurturing man fleeing before the clown arrives symbolizes her wish to flee the prospect of facing motherhood alone.

It's frightening to depend upon someone, since I'm accustomed to depending on no one.

I had a dream where I was part of an all-male militia out on a rolling green plain, under a big blue sky. At one point, I look across the plain and see this platoon of Red Coats coming at me, thousands of them. They weren't marching in a line; they were more like a mob. I said to my platoon, "We have to go. There are people coming." Then we turn around and there's a department store behind us. We're in the appliance section, surrounded by washers and refrigerators. We don't buy anything. We just run through the aisles and out the other door, then through a hall, and that's when the dream ends.

Michaela, 36, social worker

In many ways, up until now Michaela has defined herself by her independence. Since she was a teenager, she's paid her own way with minimal help from her parents. At times she barely scraped by, but her ability to live on very little has always been a source of personal pride. As an adult, it gave her the flexibility to pursue an emotionally fulfilling, if not financially rewarding, career. There have been times when Michaela's bohemian lifestyle forced her to face difficult issues, like whether or not she would be able to support a child.

Now, for the first time in her adult life, Michaela is far from alone. She has a caring partner and a baby on the way. It's a good time for Michaela, yet given her history, she can't help but worry that her partner won't be there for her or their baby, and she fears that caring for a child on her own will diminish her ability to support herself. To women for whom independence is a large portion of their identity, the notion of relying on a dependable partner and caring for a dependent baby may be foreign to their experience and very frightening.

Michaela's dream begins in an idyllic setting, symbolizing her pregnancy. The image of a rolling green plain evokes growth, mirroring the growth that's occurring inside her body. The big blue sky suggests her freedom, something she cherishes but is afraid of losing once she becomes a mother. Michaela arrives on the scene in an all male platoon, a metaphor for her lifelong independence. This particular battle is to maintain a safe and secure existence, protecting her pregnancy from dangerous outside forces.

When the platoon is faced with the attacking Red Coats, she's the only one aware enough to recognize their potential threat and has no choice but to take charge of the disorderly mob of men. Taking charge is familiar to Michaela, but the life-threatening implication of the military imagery and attacking mob suggests she fears, with the added responsibility of a child, she'll have to fight harder than ever just to survive.

Closely related to Michaela's conflict between independence and the dependency of a family unit are her feelings about her sexual identity. In the dream, her only two possible identities are opposing gender stereotypes—a soldier and a housewife. It's no accident that the militia she's with is all male. She's reacting to the extreme femaleness of pregnancy and motherhood. Men don't have to worry about pregnancy, birthing, breastfeeding, and other female-only activities. She's running with the men away from domesticity, but she can't escape it; when she runs, she encounters a store full of household appliances—the embodiment of her fear that becoming a mother will force her to become the female stereotype, or in other words, utterly dependent.

As a single mother, figuring out whom I can depend upon is especially complicated.

I had one dream where my parents were going on vacation and I turned on the TV and saw on the news that a plane, which could have been their plane, had crashed. I called my sister over and started crying and being very hysterical at the possibility that they were dead. Then they called me, and I knew they were alive and well. But even after their call I was truly sad and felt like they weren't necessarily alive, they could have been calling me from the dead. Then finally it clicked a couple minutes later that they were fine. I don't think they were even on the plane.

Isabella, 29, graduate student

When Isabella became pregnant, her baby's father refused to accept responsibility for the child. Isabella was in graduate school at the time and unprepared both emotionally and financially to care for a baby by herself. The experience was so traumatic, she left school and moved home with her parents, who agreed to help her raise her child. While her parents' support is a tremendous relief for Isabella, being so dependent upon them at an age when she feels she should be more self-reliant makes her uncomfortable.

Dependency issues for single mothers can be especially difficult. While many women who choose to have a child on their own feel confident they can provide a good life for their baby, others feel that without outside assistance there will be no way for them to make it work. If you're about to be a single mother, you may also worry that if something were to happen to you there would be no one for your child to depend upon. To compensate for this, you may seek some sort of replacement for the father—relatives, friends, or perhaps a new partner.

At the beginning of her dream, it seems like Isabella's parents are simply going on vacation, but she quickly learns that in a flash they could be gone forever. For Isabella, this describes both a need and a fear: In one sense, she needs her parents to recede into the background so she doesn't have to compete with them for the role of parent to her unborn child. At the same time, since the father of the child is already gone, she fears her parents might also abandon her just when she needs them most.

When she learns her parents' plane may have crashed, she's overcome with emotion. Part of this effusion is grief over the loss of her loved ones; another part is recognizing that without her parents she has no choice but to be completely independent and step fully into the role of mother to her baby. There's no way out—in order for her to care for her child, she can no longer be a child herself.

I'm frightened by the idea of having a baby depend upon me completely.

I've had a lot of anxiety dreams involving me taking care of a small child. It's usually one of my brother's kids, and some natural disaster happens where I lose control. For example, I had a dream I was on a boat. At first it's a lovely scene. I'm on the Caribbean, the sun is shining, and I'm holding my nephew, Alex, my brother's youngest child, who's seven and very small. Then a gigantic wave comes up from behind, and I hear my brother scream, "Don't let anything happen to him!"

I reassure my nephew, "I have you! I have you!" but he doesn't seem scared. He knows that I have him, but I doubt myself. Then the wave collapses over us, and we're plunged into the water. I'm still holding Alex, but I don't know if he's drowned or what. I tell myself in the dream, "It's bad, stop it," but then I wake up and make up some ending myself like, "Oh, I saved him." But I don't know if it's true because it's unresolved. The dreams are always unresolved. Sometimes I go back to sleep and try to fix them.

When I woke up from this dream, I really felt like I had killed my brother's son, but when I closed my eyes again, I saw myself back at the scene of the accident and this time, life preservers appeared. I grabbed one, put it on my nephew, and held him while swimming furiously to shore. When we reached the beach and everything was okay, I felt like a hero. Afterwards, we sat around a campfire with my brother and I said to him, "See how we survived!"

Andrea, 30, grant writer

Until recently, Andrea was the baby in her family. Her parents had her later in life, and her siblings, all boys, were eight, ten, and twelve years older than her. Being the little one had become part of her identity. For Andrea, having a baby of her own means not only stepping out of her baby-place and defying her familial role of childlike dependence, but also accepting the responsibility of a child who will be totally dependent upon her.

Andrea's dream begins like the opening of a horror movie—the clear water, bright sun, and adorable child evoke an image too idyllic to be real, as if the scene's perfection is a sign of disaster to come. This may be what Andrea's telling herself about her pregnancy: "Don't trust the calm. Danger is lurking just around the corner."

In her dream, Andrea tries on the role of mother by taking care of her nephew, Alex, the son of the brother who helped raise her. It's with this brother that Andrea needs to work through her own conflicts about becoming a parent. When the tidal wave swells behind the boat, before she can form her own reaction, she hears her father-brother's voice screaming the command, "Don't let anything happen to him." Andrea readily admits that in the face of danger she doubted her ability to protect her nephew. Yet despite her uncertainty, she assures her brother she's dependable by telling the child in no uncertain terms, "I have you!" It's like a test where she needs her brother to judge if she's worthy of being a mother. The child's trust and utter dependence in this situation highlight Andrea's insecurity about her ability to protect.

The first part of the dream ends with Andrea in the water holding her nephew, unsure if he's alive and the question of her ability to parent still unresolved. This image is in part an allusion to the baby in her womb, which is also floating in water. The dangers surrounding childbirth are uncontrollable, and as in the dream, a wave of disaster is always a possibility.

Andrea feels competent handling the responsibilities of her daily life, but unsure of her ability to handle the responsibility of caring for a child. Her self-doubt is so disturbing to her that she couldn't rest until she established herself in her own mind as a dependable mother. She forced herself to go back to sleep and return to her drowning nephew with life preservers. When in the dream she finally transports the boy to safety, her self-image emerges radically changed. No longer the helpless little sister, Andrea is now a heroine. Her declaration, "See how we survived!" is a demonstration of her newfound confidence in the idea that a child can depend upon her, as well as the idea that she doesn't always have to depend upon her brother, or for that matter, anyone else.

Sexuality

Your changing sexual identity will undoubtedly affect how you feel about becoming a mother.

I don't know why, but since becoming pregnant I've had all sorts of sexual dreams.

I had this dream late in my pregnancy, just after I started leaking colostrum. I was hosting a party at our home, in our living room. I had made all sorts of food, and there were beautiful flowers, candles, the whole nine yards. Everything was perfect. I was wearing an elegant, formfitting cocktail dress, which means I must not have been pregnant anymore, and I happened to look pretty terrific. I'm not really sure why I went to all the trouble, since the guests weren't people I particularly cared for, mostly friends of my husband that I didn't want to invite to our wedding, and also some strangers.

The party was going very well, when suddenly my breast escaped from my dress. It started spraying wildly, like an out-of-control garden hose. Milk went squirting all over the room. There was a ton of it, so much that it splattered the walls and drapes and started collecting in puddles on the floor. It soaked every last guest, most of whom were men. I tried to regain control of my breast, but it was slip-

*pery and kept sliding out of my hands. Needless to say, it
was very embarrassing.*

Heather, 30, software designer

Sexuality and pregnancy are inextricably linked; sex
causes women to become pregnant, pregnancy changes our
bodies, and having a child changes our lives. Because of all
these changes, this is a time when the notion of your sexuality is up for revision and you may worry about how pregnancy will affect both your body and how you perceive
yourself as a sexual being. So while sexual dreams during
pregnancy can be about sex in the erotic sense, very often
they express our concerns about our changing bodies and
who we are becoming sexually.

To some degree, most of us fear the changes pregnancy
and childbirth will make to our bodies, both temporary and
permanent. Heredity may provide some indication of what
to expect, which in some cases gives little cause for comfort,
and is not necessarily what will happen to you anyway.
While you may address these fears in your waking hours,
there can be enough leftover anxiety surrounding this issue
to spill into your dreams.

During pregnancy, one of the first physical changes to
your sexual self is your rapidly growing breasts. For some
women, this exponential increase in bra size is a delight—
for others, it's a nuisance, and their growing breasts can
seem out of control. In Heather's dream, she struggles
against an unruly pregnant body to maintain the image she
had of her sexuality before pregnancy, and control over
both her physical being and the events in her life.

Heather was very pregnant when this dream occurred,
and her breasts, once a symbol of her sexuality, had just
started to leak colostrum, the fluid that forms before milk

production begins. Yet in her dream, Heather saw herself entertaining with a nonpregnant body she could show off in a slinky cocktail dress. That in the dream, and in that dress, she had to feed a group of people she either didn't know or didn't like has implications. The slinky dress suggests Heather harbors anxiety about her ability to present herself in a sexual way during her pregnancy; she even had to revert to her pre-pregnant body in order to feel and look "pretty terrific." The food imagery symbolizes her feelings about taking care of and feeding others whether she wants to or not, be it the guests at her party or the baby growing inside her.

The dream takes on humorous and nightmarish qualities when Heather's breast escapes from her dress and begins to squirt the guests, symbolizing the loss of control she feels over her changing body and changing sexuality. Heather's perfect living room can be seen as a symbol of her pre-pregnant body and her ability to present it in a sexual way. As the milk from Heather's breast begins to soak the drapes and flood the living room, it's as though her pregnant body is overtaking—even destroying—her former sexual self. With its hoselike quality and spraying ability, her breast can also be seen as the phallus that impregnated her. Soaking the guests is an aggressive action expressing a part of Heather that is angry about being pregnant and all the changes her body must endure, changes that set her apart from her husband and the male guests she entertains.

Breasts, our most public of private parts, stand out for the world to see as sexualized parts of the body that women have and men don't. During pregnancy, as our bodies change and our emotions begin to shift toward mothering, our perception of our breasts may change, too. As we imagine nursing a baby, our breasts begin to seem utilitarian. We know it will even become acceptable to expose them publicly to nurse, in part because they are no longer viewed in a sexual way. We may wonder if they will ever again be regarded as sexual, by ourselves and by others.

When contemplating breastfeeding a newborn, what woman hasn't had nightmarish thoughts about an embarrassing public exposure? What woman hasn't wondered how she will maintain a sexual existence once she becomes a mother? For Heather, as for many of us, these questions stem from the need to continue feeling desirable.

As my body changes, I worry my partner may no longer find me sexy.

I have to preface this by telling you my husband would never cheat on me—he's too afraid of me. But I had this dream where he brought a woman to our house. I was in the kitchen, still big and pregnant, but cradling a baby in my arms when he opened the door. He was smiling really hard and was accompanied by a leggy brunette who he introduced to me as Lindsey. By the way, I don't know this woman in real life.

Without another word, my husband led Lindsey by the hand to the living room couch where he started kissing and groping her, totally aware that I could see what was going on. They started really getting into it and they undressed each other and began making love.

The baby and I were forced to watch them from the kitchen door, only five feet away. I kept wanting to close my eyes, but couldn't move a muscle. I was sure he was doing this just to piss me off. And it definitely worked. I woke up mad at him and stayed mad for about a week. Poor guy.

Karen, 27, homemaker

While many men and women consider the pregnant female body sexy, it's common during pregnancy for us to feel uncertain of our desirability. This can make us feel we have lost a degree of sexual power in our relationship with our partner. Karen has always perceived her husband as too afraid to do anything like cheat on her, but now that she's pregnant, she's clearly feeling more vulnerable and less powerful than she did before.

In her dream, as Karen watches her husband and the other woman make love, she's an outsider, unable to participate and powerless to stop it. Karen experiences the pain of rejection, which makes her feel hurt and angry. She feels different from her husband, the leggy brunette, and all the other nonpregnant people who seem to be free to maintain a sexual existence—she's pregnant and the mother of a young child, unable to fool around and maybe no longer desirable. Meanwhile, fatherhood in no way diminishes her husband's sexual viability, nor does it curtail his freedom to pursue sex. Holding the baby while she witnesses this scene underscores Karen's fear the baby will get in the way of her relationship with her husband and that once she becomes a mother, he won't see her in a sexual way anymore.

Being pregnant and having the baby simultaneously suggests that Karen may have feelings of ambivalence about becoming a mother and that she wishes she were the sexy brunette on the couch instead of the mother standing apart in the kitchen. The dream ends with Karen asserting that her husband was attempting to make her angry, but underneath that feeling is the worry that he's actually angry at her for changing.

Sometimes I dream about my single days, when sex still felt like an adventure.

I've had this dream three times. I'm attending a conference in a house in New England—a clapboard kind of Cape Cod house, but big, like the one in The House of the Seven Gables. *My body, even though I'm pregnant, is slimmer than it is now, and I have long hair. I feel like an earthy, beautiful goddess—a man's ideal vision of what a pregnant woman is like. I'm very pregnant, but still very desirable and hot.*

My ex-boyfriend is there, and he looks really cute. A colleague of mine locks us in a room together and we start making out. The next thing you know, there's sexy music playing, and we start to do it. And I mean really do it. We're having experimental, kinky sex, complete with toys and even a little tying up. Then I'm like, "Oh, my God, I'm married!" Inevitably, what happens is the next day, I go back to my husband, admit the whole thing to him, and he divorces me.

Elena, 34, advertising executive

Elena and her husband married after a brief courtship, and she became pregnant within their first year of marriage. In less than two years, she went from being a single woman to a married, expectant mother. This abrupt change to her sexual identity has left her reeling. Elena's dream is an attempt to reconcile her old life with her new one; she clearly misses the excitement she attaches to the idea of her former sexual self.

Although the setting for Elena's dream is a professional conference she's attending with colleagues, the atmosphere seems more like a house party thrown by teenagers whose parents are away. The presence of Elena's ex-boyfriend expresses a longing to return to her single days when sex was an adventure. That she's on a business trip away from her husband implies she feels she had to get away from him and from her current life in order to reconnect with her carefree sexual self.

When a colleague locks Elena and her ex-boyfriend together in a room, it's reminiscent of Seven Minutes in Heaven and other sexual games teenagers play. Elena is trying to recapture a time when she felt her sexuality was validated, and she wishes her husband made her feel as desirable as her ex-boyfriend does in her dream. That he doesn't angers her. When she confesses her liaison to him, it's not as though she's seeking forgiveness—it's an aggressive act of defiance. She almost seems relieved when her confession results in divorce, as though he's given her permission to revert to her pre-pregnancy state when she felt desirable, desired, and free.

For many of us, a negative emotional side of commitment is the feeling of entrapment and that certain sexual doors must now close. Becoming pregnant and having a baby can make us feel like those doors have been locked and the keys thrown away. Elena's dream expresses these feelings; she's locked in a room the way she sometimes feels locked into marriage, and perhaps into a sexual identity she has difficulty relating to. The "little bit of tying up" not only expresses Elena's longing for exotic sexual adventure, but also implies that as a mother, she'll be irrevocably tied to her husband and her child.

Elena also feels trapped in her pregnant body and expresses dissatisfaction with it in her dream. In order to feel desirable, she must be a slim, longhaired goddess, not unlike the pregnant actresses and supermodels proudly displaying their swelling yet perfect bodies on the covers of magazines. On some level, Elena believes that men, including her husband, can find a pregnant woman desirable only if she adheres to that image. The large house in the dream can be seen as a stand-in for Elena's perception of her growing body as being literally big as a house, not at all the ideal she holds in her mind.

Pregnancy teaches us that sexuality is as much about affirmation of our physical attractiveness as it is about intimacy. Take, for example, the unsolicited comments women receive from men on the street. As much as we may dislike these comments and find them intrusive, when they suddenly disappear, we may miss them, or at least their affirmation of our physical appearance. Once you're visibly pregnant, you may notice that remarks about your attractiveness are replaced by comments about the baby, and you may wonder, "Where did I go?" In fact, the world treats a pregnant woman like she's so sexless, complete strangers think it's okay to reach out and touch their bellies.

Can I be a good mother and still keep the sexual part of myself?

I dreamt I was at my obstetrician's office for my appointment. I must have already had the baby, because I wasn't pregnant anymore. Anyway, there was an intense attraction between us (he is a little too cute in real life), and we started having sex.

Afterwards, I was pulling myself together and went to the mirror to put my makeup on, and the reflection in the mirror wasn't my face—it was my baby's. My hair was also like baby hair—thin and fine and in two pigtails. I was trying to put makeup on these infant features, and I wondered if my skin might be too sensitive, since it was baby skin.

My doctor started speaking to me arrogantly, and sud-

denly I felt remorse for what had just happened, not because I had committed adultery, but because my doctor turned out to be just another asshole guy.

Mia, 34, accessories buyer

When we think of doctors, we think of authority figures. Even outside the medical profession, the word connotes having attained the highest degree of knowledge in a given field. We may view our obstetrician not just as an authority figure when it comes to pregnancy, but as the one who will literally give us our baby. We may be awestruck by our doctor's possession of seemingly mysterious knowledge and, especially if our doctor's male, develop a little crush, even if we're not consciously attracted to him. If our doctor is a woman, we may regard her as an idealized sister or mother figure.

It should come as no surprise that your obstetrician can surface in your dreams, and that those dreams are often of a sexual nature. The relationship between a woman and her obstetrician is extremely intimate. Your doctor has, after all, seen and touched the most private parts of your body. The intimate nature of the touching is smoothed over by professional protocol, making it seem absurd to consider the examination even remotely sexual. Yet during such an emotionally charged time as pregnancy, it's normal to look to those around you—especially authority figures like doctors—for support and affirmation of your desirability and worth. As with any intimate relationship, you would naturally hope the appreciation is reciprocal.

Mia consciously recognizes her attraction to her doctor, and in her dream, she explores the possibility that the attraction might be mutual. In the dream he's attracted to her, to the point of breaching professional protocol to have sex with her, giving Mia the sexual validation she craves in her waking hours. The doctor also represents her husband, and her need to still be desired and appreciated by him, as well.

Mia's reversion to her pre-pregnant body expresses her ongoing struggle with her sexual identity. She's also wondering if her doctor will still want to see her after her baby's born. It's normal to grow accustomed and even look forward to your visits with your obstetrician—after all, he's the one who can truly reassure you about the baby. By the last weeks of your pregnancy, you may be seeing your doctor daily—probably more often than you see your closest friends. The relationship culminates with the baby's delivery, not only one of the most emotional experiences of a woman's life, but also one in which so much faith and trust is put into another person, her doctor.

Although Mia states she didn't feel guilty in the dream for her extramarital activity, when she goes to the mirror to fix her makeup, the baby makes itself known. With its fine hair and sensitive skin functioning as metaphors for Mia feeling vulnerable and sensitive, the baby reminds Mia that she's still pregnant, that pregnancy is the reason for her questioning her sexual identity, and that as her child, it does not approve of her behavior. The baby's presence represents Mia's guilty conscience, implying that by having sex, she's merely taking care of her own needs. (On a literal level, it points to the anxiety some couples have about the possibility their unborn baby can somehow sense what's going on during intercourse.) Unconsciously, she feels she's not permitted to do that—her sexual self must be put aside in order to be a proper mother to her baby. Mia's transformed image in the mirror symbolizes a new awareness of aspects of herself that, before now, have been unknown or unacceptable to her.

Is sexual imagery in my dreams always about sex?

I need to preface this dream by telling you that while I have the utmost respect and admiration for my obstetrician as both a doctor and a human being, I am in no way attracted to him. Well, maybe I am because this is what I dreamt about him.

I was at his office for my checkup. I was far along in my pregnancy, and my stomach looked and felt enormous. I was waiting for him in the examination room, wearing one of those ultra-attractive disposable blue paper gowns. After waiting for what seemed like an eternity, my doctor came in the room and smiled at me. There was definitely something different in his manner, and he said, "You know, you're my only patient who actually looks good in one of those gowns." I was flattered by the compliment, especially since I looked like such a cow.

Then his nurse came into the room. It wasn't his real nurse, but this busty blonde with lots of cleavage, like a nurse in a porn film would look. She smiled and locked the door, then came over to me and took off my gown. I thought, "Oh, my God, they want to have sex with me!" and I felt reluctant—not because I didn't want to, but because I was afraid that the receptionist and the other patients would barge in on us.

My doctor must have read my mind and told me it was okay, which gave me the impression the rest of the staff was in on it and that it happened all the time. They started having sex with me, and all I could think about was whether or not they did this with every patient, which made me feel like I wasn't really special to him after all.

Christina, 35, florist

While dreams are repositories for forbidden thoughts, like a good novel or film, their meanings are often rooted in their subtext. On the surface, Christina's dream about her doctor may seem similar to Mia's, but while sexual feelings are clearly present in this dream, its underlying subject is Christina's need to be taken care of and understood. The sexual components of this dream, though they may be the most outstanding, are used as a stage for acting out a far more elaborate set of issues.

In her dream, Christina is very pregnant and concerned about her sexual attractiveness. Her pregnancy has changed her sex life with her husband, and she's worried it won't return to normal after the baby arrives. The lack of physical affirmation within her marriage makes her think maybe her husband doesn't love her as much as he used to and that he's sorry they got into this situation in the first place. In the dream, the doctor is her savior. He understands pregnant women and can even read her mind. He appreciates her, compliments her, and wants to have sex with her. He gives her exactly what she longs for—physical and emotional care.

On another level, the dream can be read as a metaphor for Christina's dependency issues, with the doctor-and-nurse team representing Christina's parents. Christina's mother and father took care of her needs unconditionally. Now she's wondering whether she'll be able to understand and take care of her baby as well as her parents took care of her as a child, and her obstetrician is taking care of her during her pregnancy. At the end of the dream, Christina realizes though her obstetrician makes her feel special, she's just one in an ongoing stream of women who come to him with the same issue. This insight made her feel guilty not only about having extramarital sex, but for being so needy, as well.

Some of my pregnant friends tell me they have dreams about sex—but not me.

Early in my pregnancy, just after I learned I was having twins, I dreamt somebody was stabbing me in the stomach with a screwdriver. I don't know where I was—I just know I felt something—not pain, more like a sensation. I looked down and saw a hand penetrating my stomach with a screwdriver. I couldn't see who was doing it, but there was blood everywhere, pools of it, real gore. I woke up afraid I had hurt the babies. I remember thanking God it was just a dream.

Tracy, 28, medical biller

While Tracy's dream may seem devoid of sexual imagery, it's very much about sex and its consequences. Sex for Tracy used to be just for pleasure. It was an expression of the intimacy, love, and desire that colored her marriage. And until recently, there were no consequences—that is, until she conceived. While a literal interpretation of the screwdriver penetrating Tracy's stomach can be fear of undergoing a C-section, it's also a representation, albeit a negative one, of the phallus and the sex act that made her become pregnant.

Upon learning she was having twins, Tracy's outward reaction was one of joyful surprise, but her unconscious feelings about having two babies at once weren't quite so positive. Her dream expresses her anger toward her husband, who with his "screwdriver," made her twice as pregnant as she'd planned to be. For Tracy, the idea of having twins feels like it might be too much.

When Tracy had this dream, pregnancy had already begun to change her life. Between nausea, hormone-induced mood swings, and swollen, tender breasts, her unconscious wish, as depicted by the image of a stabbing screwdriver, was to eradicate her pregnancy. In this instance, the screwdriver is a weapon, and the violence, Tracy's fears. That an anonymous hand in an unidentifiable space wields the weapon is Tracy's way of denying she could harbor such an unacceptable wish, even subconsciously. Yet after she woke up, Tracy felt relieved, not because she realized she hadn't been stabbed, but because her babies had not been harmed.

During pregnancy, the mystery of what's going on inside us and our inability to predict the exact outcome can cause tremendous anxiety. It is, therefore, not unusual to worry about all kinds of things. A common concern for some women and their partners, though usually unfounded, is that intercourse or climaxing might somehow harm the baby. In that respect, the phallic screwdriver penetrating Tracy represents her fear of sex as potentially harmful to her unborn babies.

Since becoming pregnant, I feel sexier than ever.

In the beginning of my last trimester, I had a dream where I was lying in bed with my husband beside me, and flowers were growing from my vagina. I think they were Gerber daisies, which would make sense, because they bring back pleasant memories of a trip I took to Africa.

I was so amazed at the beautiful way the flowers came out. In a slow and fluid movement, their stems just sort of grew tall with closed bulbs that unfolded, then opened up really wide. I like vibrant colors and these flowers left me breathless with their petals striped in bright hues of yellow, fuchsia, red, and orange. I woke up because I was nearly brought to tears by the beauty of the dream.

Amanda, 39, restaurant manager

The good news is that for many women, pregnancy is accompanied by a libidinous streak that may rival—or even surpass—anything they had been accustomed to before conceiving. There are both physical and emotional reasons for this. Some doctors believe the increased blood supply in the pelvic area and increased hormones in the body can intensify the sensations a pregnant woman experiences during lovemaking. The possible emotional reasons for this increase in sexual desire and responsiveness are more varied.

While heightened sexual feelings during pregnancy can be a way for us to deny the changes occurring in our bodies and our lives—and perhaps an attempt to preserve our pre-pregnant sexual selves—for many of us, it's precisely these changes that make us feel more sexual. Many women—and their partners—find the swelling breasts and bellies of pregnancy to be the height of femininity, as well as an exciting novelty, and a sexual turn-on in their own right. Pregnancy can deepen intimacy in many ways and may bring with it an increased sexual closeness. And for many of us, not having to worry about birth control for once brings with it a new sense of freedom.

Amanda's dream combines elements of her past sexual identity, her evolving identity as a mother, and her changing body into a personal narrative about her body's ability to create life—literally to flower. That the flowers are Gerber daisies relates back to Amanda's trip to Africa, an exotic locale that holds memories of a positive time in her life. The image of the flowers with their long stalklike stems is undoubtedly phallic—their movements evoke intercourse, and Amanda's breathlessness from their beauty can be seen as a metaphor for orgasm. In the dream, Amanda's sexual activity seems masturbatory; her husband is beside her but not participating. She's feeling good about her pregnant body and feeling sexually complete within herself.

Whatever your level of sexual activity and desire may be during pregnancy, your sexuality is clearly not put on a shelf for nine months. And although exploring sexual issues may be uncomfortable and even embarrassing, it will undoubtedly be useful in helping redefine who you are as you become a mother.

SECTION TWO

YOUR RELATIONSHIPS

During pregnancy, you're beginning to define yourself in a whole new way. But this doesn't happen in a vacuum—you're also redefining who you are in relation to the people in your life.

As you prepare to become a mother and your priorities begin to shift, it's normal to wonder if your relationships will change, and in what ways. Meanwhile, others are beginning to see you differently, which can be unsettling if you're no longer sure of how you see yourself. You may feel uncomfortable in both your old and new roles, since it's difficult to know who you'll be as a partner, lover, family member, friend, or colleague or how your role in these relationships will change once your baby's born.

And as all these relationships evolve, you're also beginning to form a brand-new and incredibly important relationship—the one with your baby. Even before your baby's born, this relationship is bound to stir up all kinds of feelings and issues about who your baby will be and what you'll be like as its mother.

Your Relationship with Your Partner

*As you and your partner evolve into parents,
your relationship is evolving, too.*

Having a baby with my partner makes me feel connected to him in a whole new way.

Early in my second pregnancy I dreamt I had a girl. We had her on the kitchen table in a baby seat, and she looked exactly like my husband. She had these very manly features, and I was like, "Oh, they would really look a lot better on a boy." I know this sounds awful, but I was so glad when I had a boy because I thought our combined genetics wouldn't produce the most feminine features in the world. I was really worried that if we had a girl she would need a little work here or there. My husband has a large, beakish nose and these big recessed eyes—exaggerated features. Put it all together on him, it looks great. Put it all together on a baby girl, and it's like, ewww! We were all looking at her thinking, "Oh, well, she'll do." But she was really ugly and kind of a disappointment.

Sherry, 41, teacher

The relationship most profoundly affected when you have a baby is the one with your partner. As you evolve into parents, you realize your relationship is evolving, too, since together you're bringing a new life into the world, the fundamental creative act. Having a baby can make you feel especially connected to one another—it brings with it the hope and expectation that by sharing such a special experience you'll deepen your relationship and strengthen your commitment. Perhaps even more than marriage, having a child with someone brings with it a sense of permanence; no matter what may happen between the two of you, you'll both be your child's parents forever.

At some time or other, most of us have fantasized about having the perfect child. Yet when we look critically at our partner and ourselves and imagine what kind of baby we would make together, we may worry about the result of our particular blend of genes. Sometimes these kinds of thoughts are simply about what your baby will be like, but they can also reveal other kinds of concerns. On the surface, Sherry's dream is about her fear of having an ugly baby. But it's also a complex picture of what it means to her to deepen her commitment to her partner, as well as a way for her to question if she's really prepared for him to be not just her husband, but the father of her child as well.

When you first met your partner and as your relationship developed, you probably took stock of his qualities. You may have asked yourself, "Am I attracted to him? Is he smart? Does he have a job?" Now that you're having a baby together, these kinds of questions are probably emerging again—this time with a different significance attached to them, since by having a baby, you're not only creating a life, you're also inviting your partner into a new and incredibly important role. This concept can take some getting used to.

I'm afraid my partner won't share in the day-to-day responsibilities of caring for our baby.

My husband and I were riding the local train to Brooklyn for a dentist appointment. I had this blue pillow I've been carrying since I became pregnant. I was also holding my husband's bag and his jacket. When we got to Brooklyn, he went to look for the express train while I waited on the local.

While he was gone, the door to the local closed and we got separated. I knew I would find him at the dentist, so I just continued on to the office, which was located near an agency dedicated to protecting children against abuse, where I used to work. In the dream, I didn't actually have an appointment for my teeth. It turned out to be for a sonogram showing that inside my baby's skull there was no brain.

Jillian, 39, computer programmer

When we marry, little by little we can fall into gender-role stereotypes harking back to the days of *Ozzie and Harriet*—stereotypes we would outright reject in other areas of our lives. A single woman who's a whiz with a power drill turns it over to her husband moments after they've crossed the threshold. And once married, a man who'd managed to do his own laundry can no longer even match his own socks. Now that you're pregnant, this shift in roles, which may have been so gradual it was barely perceptible, can feel like an avalanche. No matter what else is going on in your life, you know you're the one expected to take on the traditional role as the baby's primary caregiver.

Jillian's dream explores her feelings not only about becoming a mother, but about the changing dynamics of her relationship with her husband, as well. She was in her seventh month when she dreamt about being left alone on the train. By this time, she was feeling heavy and slow, and it upset her to realize her life would continue to be slowed down after the baby's birth.

Jillian's husband has always put in long hours at work. This never bothered her much when it was just the two of them, but now she fears that for the most part, she'll be left alone with the burden of caring for their newborn. Her old workplace, an agency for abused children, connotes her conflict about whether to stay home with the baby or return to work. On some level, she believes if she chooses to put in the kind of hours at work her husband does, without reprisal, she'll feel like she's neglecting, or even abusing, their child.

In her dream, getting separated from her husband reveals Jillian's fear she must travel alone through so many aspects of motherhood. She's scared she'll be left behind on the slow train, holding the bag, or in other words, the pregnancy, while her husband is unencumbered by pregnancy's physical demands—or even by his own belongings. He's able to escape on life's express train and rapidly move ahead on his own. When Jillian is left carrying her husband's stuff, she worries she won't just be left to care for their baby, but that she'll be taking care of him, too.

Although Jillian worries about being abandoned by her husband, she actually relies upon him as a tremendous source of support and comfort. In her dream, this aspect of her husband is symbolized by the pillow. Jillian has carried this pillow throughout her pregnancy and just as she knows it will make her a little more comfortable wherever she is, she also knows she can lean on her husband to support her and cushion any blows that may come her way. Similarly, his jacket, which also remains with her throughout the dream, can be seen as a symbol of his protection.

Toward the end of the dream, what began benignly enough as a trip to the dentist turns into an obstetrician appointment where Jillian's greatest fear is realized, a fear shared by so many older expectant mothers in particular— that they've waited too long and their bodies won't be able to carry a baby to term. The image of the empty skull is also a projection of Jillian's fears about herself. She's questioning what will happen to her relationship if her husband continues to interact with the rest of the world while she's mainly occupied in the nursery. She fears she won't have anything interesting to contribute to her relationship and that her husband will regard her as dull and brainless.

I worry that the pressure of providing for a child will adversely affect our relationship.

My husband and I live in New York in a SoHo loft, and the rent has gone up to about a zillion dollars a month. However, we can't leave because there's nothing we could find for the money that's the same size. So we have to have a roommate, Peter, who I absolutely cannot stand and whose presence I completely resent. But he's willing to fork over a thousand dollars a month for a bedroom with no windows, so I have to grin and bear it.

Here's the dream I had about him. I was in bed sleeping. I started stirring, and I realized my husband was trying to wake me up by going down on me. It felt great, and I was just kind of going with it for a while, becoming more and more aroused while in a half-sleep state. Then, I looked down at my husband's head and was horrified to discover it was the bleached-blond head of my roommate, who I am so repulsed by I can't adequately describe it. But despite my revulsion for him, I was too turned on to make him stop and get off me. I came and was instantly filled with guilt and shame for allowing it to happen.

Camille, 36, theater manager

Camille's dream captures more than a pregnant woman's concern about feeling sexually desired by her partner; it captures the quintessential New York concern about having an affordable apartment that's bigger than a phone booth—or in other words, concerns about money. No matter where you live or what's going on in your life, finances can be a significant source of stress in your relationship. With a baby comes the fiscal double whammy of soaring expenses at a time when you might actually want to work less.

The dream is a metaphor for Camille's feelings of entrapment. Like many of us during pregnancy, Camille feels trapped in her body. It makes her tired and uncomfortable. Camille also feels trapped by the need to board a despised roommate. His presence causes her to feel like she's prostituting herself, that she has to "grin and bear" his intrusion on her marriage for money. In her dream, her husband sleeps right through it, suggesting she thinks he won't be able to provide for their growing family or for her sexual and emotional needs.

Camille also worries that her husband doesn't feel as attracted to her anymore and that they'll never have sex like they used to. She's angry with him for not showing her enough sexual attention. In fact, she's angry with him for not showing her enough attention at all. Camille wants to feel desired by her husband, but instead of confronting the issue directly, in her dream, she turns to the other accessible male in her life—her roommate. Her guilt at the end of the dream largely results from her realization that through her actions she has humiliated both herself and her husband, something she would never do in real life.

The roommate also represents forbidden and very unmaternal desires and feelings, like having sex just for the fun of it, as well as negative emotions, like rage. But most of all, the roommate represents an intruder—he doesn't belong in Camille's home, and he certainly doesn't belong in her marital bed.

The roommate's presence as a sexual partner is not so much about sexuality as it is about Camille's concern over how the baby might intrude on her relationship with her husband. She knows once she gives birth, she'll have to give of herself to her baby unconditionally, and even when she's not in the mood, she'll have to grin and bear it. She wants to know if the baby will always be in bed with them.

I worry that my partner will abandon me, just when I need him most.

Since becoming pregnant I've had a couple of dreams about my husband cheating on me. In these dreams, we're always young, college-age, which is strange because I didn't meet my husband until years after leaving school. We're not married, either. We are, however, always in our current home. In these dreams, he tells me he wants to break up with me because he's fallen in love with someone else.

Jennifer, 29, investment banker

During pregnancy, the rapid changes occurring in our bodies and in our lives can make even the most self-confident among us feel insecure in a way we haven't since we were teenagers. When we're unsure of how we feel about ourselves, it's normal to question how our partner perceives us and to wonder if they even want to be with us at all. So it makes sense that when Jennifer dreamt about her husband falling in love with another woman, they were once again college-age.

Pregnancy and college days are both times when you're on the verge of major life changes. But unlike pregnancy, during college, your options can seem unlimited. Important choices—where you'll live, what kind of work you'll do, and who you'll be with—are probably not yet set in stone. Now that Jennifer's married and about to have a baby, she's aware of how some of her options are closing off, which sometimes makes her feel trapped. Jennifer's scared that if she's having these kinds of feelings, her husband must be having them, too. She worries that instead of becoming a father, he'd rather return to a time of fewer responsibilities and commitments, when acting on his desires had little consequence. When Jennifer imagines him indulging this wish and possibly leaving her alone to raise their baby, she's asking an important question: "Now that becoming a father means making a stronger commitment to our marriage, does my husband have one foot out the door in a place where he's free from family life?"

I love my husband—so why do I keep dreaming about my old boyfriend?

Since my eighth month, I've had dreams where I've had the baby and it's wonderful. In these dreams, I'm at home with my husband eating dinner in our apartment. After taking a bite of salmon, I put down my fork and say to him in a very deadpan manner, "Ouch, I have a labor pain." The next thing you know, the dream cuts to domestic bliss, and I'm feeding the baby. The only glitch is right after that, I find out the baby's real father is my ex-boyfriend.

Linda, 34, ticket broker

Thinking—even dreaming—of an old love doesn't necessarily mean you intend to rekindle that flame. It's more likely a reaction to the magnitude of the commitments you're entering into. Now that you're starting a family, stability and permanence within your relationship are probably more important to you than ever. The paradox is, once you've attained this with your partner, you might also feel constricted. One reaction is to romanticize and long for past relationships, which we may remember, correctly or not, as more exciting than what we have now.

Linda met her husband, Jeff, on a blind date. They were together just a year before becoming engaged, and after they married, decided to have children right away. In less than two years, Jeff went from being her boyfriend, to her husband, to the father of her child. At each turn, Linda barely had the opportunity to adjust to their changing roles before their life together would go through yet another dramatic change. Now that she's pregnant, Linda appreciates the stability of her relationship, but has trouble giving over to it fully. A way of distancing herself is to escape in her lingering feelings about what she perceives to be the more exotic single life she left behind.

Many of us feel guilty when we question a relationship that's supposed to be eternal. We can feel pressure to make a marriage work for the sake of the children, even before there is a child. Linda's dream expresses her hope that a baby will solidify her relationship with her husband, yet it reveals a genteel distance between them bordering on a lack of connection. When she learns her baby's real father is her ex-boyfriend, her fantasy of domestic bliss gives way to another fantasy of having both the baby and the freedom to indulge with boyfriends as she pleases, as well as the fear of retribution for even having these thoughts.

It's hard to imagine my partner as a father— sometimes he seems more like my child.

After I learned I was having a girl, I had a lot of dreams about protecting my sister's two-year-old daughter. She's small and has curly black hair and the cutest baby face. The most vivid of these dreams took place at a party, where I saw my niece sitting alone on a staircase pouring flour all over herself.

I sensed the party was a dangerous place for her and rushed to her aid. But I soon got the feeling it was actually a dangerous place for me, because when I brushed the flour off her face, she turned out to be my husband.

I took my pint-size husband and ran out of the party into the street. I didn't know where I was and still sensed danger, but I knew I had to take care of my husband, because physically he was still a baby.

Terri, 31, physical therapist

In relationships, women often take on the role of primary nurturer. We tend to be the ones who make sure the home is in order, and we tend to take care of our partner, too. When imagining the added responsibility of caring for a new baby, we may suddenly realize just how much caretaking we actually do. At times, it can feel like too much to handle, and we may hope our partner will pitch in more, or at the very least, take care of himself.

Terri's especially accustomed to herself in the role of caretaker. In addition to having provided emotional support for her husband, she's financially supported him through medical school ever since they began living together. In fact, she'll still be supporting him until just before her due date, when he's expected to finally begin his residency. After all these years, it's difficult for Terri to imagine relinquishing any part of the caretaker role to her husband, or to believe he will truly be able to handle it.

By taking care of the little girl in her dream, Terri is giving herself over to the concept of mothering, and in doing so, makes her frightening discovery. Carrying around a pint-size husband speaks volumes about how Terri imagines her role and her relationship will change, once it includes a real baby. She's not just anticipating mothering a newborn, she feels on some level, her husband is a baby, too, and requires mothering. Since a baby can't care for a baby, she worries he'll be an ineffectual parent, and a burden on top of that. By casting her husband as a child, she's also wondering how they can possibly have an adult relationship. All of which adds up to a sense of danger for Terri— how will she be able to accept her husband as a father if she can't even accept him as a man?

Will our relationship ever return to the way it was?

My husband and I are not having sex now, but I'm thinking about sex a lot. It reminds me of when I was younger and still a virgin. On New Year's Eve, we were in our house having a party. I went to sleep at 12:30, earlier than everyone else, and started having this dream. I was in the same bed as I was sleeping in, in the same cold room, and my husband came upstairs and we were making love. It was so vivid, and just like real life, except it was a dream.

Ingrid, 28, photo editor

Beginning with the simple idea that your twosome is about to become a threesome, during pregnancy couples start to realize the kinds of intimacy they were accustomed to, sexual and otherwise, may never be quite the same. Sometimes this is by choice. Some women feel a need to create some physical and emotional distance from their husband in order to focus on the baby and on the changes they're experiencing within themselves. Others may choose to abstain from sex during pregnancy because they perceive it might not be good for them or the baby, or because their doctors have instructed them to abstain for medical reasons.

By the third trimester, for many couples, sex can seem like a distant memory. Your experience may be like Ingrid's, where so much is going on emotionally and physically, there's nothing left to devote to your sexuality. For Ingrid and her husband, sex became more sporadic and then stopped altogether. This arrangement grew from her own feelings and needs. As Ingrid's body has changed, she's become uncomfortable within it and uncomfortable with the idea of herself as a sexual being. As a result, she's ignored this side of herself completely, but feelings of desire have made their way into her dreams. The absence of a sexual relationship with her husband stirs feelings in Ingrid reminiscent of virginity, a time when she had sexual feelings but didn't act upon them.

As her dream shows, Ingrid's not entirely comfortable with the distance this has created between her and her husband. She fears once the baby arrives, this distance will not only be exacerbated, but also that they may never have sex again. Although Ingrid hopes for the return of the passion and closeness she and her husband once enjoyed, she currently lacks the motivation to do anything about it.

I'm nervous about facing motherhood without a partner.

Because I'm not with the father and he kind of left, I've had several dreams about him, especially in the beginning. The dreams are always about him coming back and me accepting it. I remember being upset about the fact I so readily took him back. In the dreams we're together and working at our relationship. There are usually problems—he's been with someone else, he's late, et cetera. It's never just fabulous when he walks in. There's always something else involved that's nagging at me. Still I'm always acting like everything's okay, I can forgive him, we can be happy, and I'm telling him we can get past it.

Shelly, 27, sales manager

Going through pregnancy without a partner to share it with can be lonely and exhausting. When you come home at night, there may be no one to help you in even the smallest ways. Thinking about the work and responsibility caring for your baby will entail can seem unmanageable and overwhelming. On top of that, the idea of not having a partner with whom you can share milestones, like your baby's first smiles and steps, can be bittersweet—you have your baby, but not the family you may have always imagined would come with it.

Many women choose to get pregnant on their own, or to go ahead with an unplanned pregnancy. They may be looking forward to single motherhood and proud of the idea that they can raise a child by themselves. That's not to say it isn't scary at times. Those of us who have chosen this path may worry we're missing out on part of the experience by not sharing it with a partner and that we might really need someone to help us through. But on some level, since we've decided to take on the role of single mother, we've also decided to take on the difficult feelings and issues that accompany that role. This isn't necessarily the case when the situation is thrust upon us by a partner who leaves, as it was on Shelly.

Shelly had these dreams in the beginning of her pregnancy, when she was feeling very vulnerable. Breaking up with her boyfriend, Rob, was difficult enough, but coupled with the stress of her pregnancy and the prospect of being a single mother, it felt like too much for her to bear. Even though she knows Rob isn't the kind of man she can rely upon, or the kind of man she wants spend her life with, part of Shelly wishes he'd come back. Like someone who stays in a bad marriage for the sake of her child, in her dreams, Shelly keeps letting Rob back into her life because she's afraid of taking care of her baby by herself, and worried about her baby not having a consistent father in its life. She lets her guard down, thinking it would be so much easier if Rob were around. Yet each time she lets him in, she feels disappointed in herself.

Shelly's pregnancy is a constant reminder of the rejection she experienced in her relationship. She's angry with Rob for abandoning her when she needed him most, yet dreams about reconnecting with him so she won't have to feel the pain of rejection anymore. By taking him back in her dreams, Shelly's trading her embarrassment about his rejection of her, which she feels her pregnancy broadcasts, for the private humiliation of accepting him, no matter what.

Your Relationship with Your Baby

*It begins long before your baby's born,
as you imagine who your baby will be and
what you'll be like together.*

Will I be able to love my baby, no matter what?

I was in my kitchen, which was beautiful, sunny, and white, and a huge monster was trying to break through the wall. It was big, disgusting, and slimy, like the creature in the movie Alien. *I was terrified and didn't know what to do, but then I saw a bowl of cat food on the floor and decided to try to feed it. The monster's claw was breaking through from beneath the wall, so I shoved some food under and stepped back. Suddenly, the creature broke through the wall, and while it was still hideous, it was much smaller than before. I realized it needed me, and that I had to take care of it. It jumped into my arms, and it felt okay.*

Nina, 36, film location scout

Your relationship with your baby starts the moment you find out you're pregnant. At this point, it's difficult to imagine your baby as a separate person. Still, you're beginning to have feelings for it. During pregnancy, there's a closeness and intimacy between you and your baby that can be experienced at no other time, in no other way, with no other person. As your pregnancy develops, so does this relationship.

Your daydreams about your baby are often pleasant ones about who it will be, what it will look like, and what you'll be like together. These fantasies help you begin to develop a relationship with your baby, and they often spill over into the dreams you have at night, where you can work out the more frightening aspects of relationship issues. Of course, your dreams are not the only way you develop a relationship with your baby—it happens by hearing its heartbeat, feeling its movements, seeing sonograms, and watching your belly grow. But what makes dreams special is that they're a place where you can practice being a mother and explore your feelings about it, including the ones you'd rather not admit—even to yourself.

The anticipation of a new baby in your life is filled with excitement, delight, and wonder, but at times it can also feel overwhelming and unmanageable. These kinds of emotional extremes are pretty much the norm of pregnancy, and in Nina's dream, they're played out in the contrast between her beautiful sun-drenched kitchen and the slimy alien.

Since you don't have any tangible evidence about who your baby will be, you're forced to try and create it in your mind. Sometimes you may imagine an adorable cherub, at others, you may worry your baby will be less than perfect. In Nina's dream, she takes this anxiety to an extreme and imagines the ultimate baby monster, just like the horrifying creature in the movie *Alien*.

Nina's slimy alien initially seems unmanageable, but when she's challenged with loving and taking care of the creature, she rises to the occasion. Even though she would have preferred a baby that was, well, human, she feeds the alien, and while it frightens her, she holds it in her arms and is able to bond with it. The dream helps her begin to feel confident that she'll be able to accept and take care of her baby, no matter what.

Will I be able to bond with my baby, even though I've never considered myself the maternal type?

I was in a large auditorium attending a dog and cat show with some friends. I'm not particularly a pet person, and I was only there because my friends were enthusiastic about it. People had come from all over the globe to have their pets' collars fitted with special translation boxes. These boxes weren't designed to translate human language into dog or cat language, but to translate English into the dog or cat's native tongue. So, if you had a German Shepherd, the box would translate English into German, into Siamese if you had a Siamese cat, and so forth.

I confided to one of my friends that I felt out of place there because I didn't have a cat or a dog, and she said, "Of course you do—you have a cat. How could you have forgotten?" So I started looking all over for it, which was stupid since I had no idea what it even looked like. But I made the effort in order to show my friend I wasn't an awful person.

I was about to give up looking when someone came up to me and told me he found my cat. I looked at it and was extremely disappointed—it was mangy-looking with matted, curly black hair, sort of like human hair, and it wasn't the least bit cute. But I had to take it because it was mine.

Cheryl, 37, attorney

Before having a baby, motherhood can seem like a club whose members have a mysterious knowledge the rest of us don't possess. You may be aware of the more obvious aspects of motherhood, like feeding the baby and changing its diapers, but the nuances of how you're going to actually relate to your baby can be bewildering—especially if you've never considered yourself to be the maternal type.

Cheryl has never felt compelled to coo at every passing carriage. She's not even sure she likes babies, and certainly has little idea how she'll respond to her own once it arrives. She recognizes that the combined forces of her expectant friends, her friends and relatives who already have children, and her biological clock, as well as her husband's eagerness to start a family, have pushed her to have a baby a little sooner than she felt ready to. It's not that she doesn't want a baby, she's just unsure how she's going to understand and relate to it. Like many first-time mothers, she feels she'll need someone or something to help translate the situation—to explain what all those infant sounds mean, what the baby needs, and how to fulfill those needs.

By describing herself as "not a pet person," and implying she's only attending the pet show because of peer pressure, Cheryl's questioning her feelings about having a baby. She feels out of place at the show without a cat or dog, and when she finds out she does in fact have a cat, she doesn't even remember it exists. The embarrassment she feels in front of her friend makes her worry about how she'll be viewed as a mother, and when she does finally look for her cat, it's only for the sake of her public persona.

The absence of a relationship between Cheryl and her cat, as well as her reluctance to forge one, further describes her conflict about having a baby. In some ways, Cheryl's the one who's lost, rather than the cat. She feels disoriented as she tries to understand how to be a mother, like her friends.

She thinks she has to figure this out by herself; she's confused and hopes someone will help her.

How you feel about your relationship with your partner may also affect your relationship with your baby. If you imagine he's not going to be there for you, the idea of coping with a baby can be overwhelming. In this sense, the man in the dream who returns Cheryl's cat represents her husband. By giving her the cat and leaving her alone to figure out what to do with it, he's enacting Cheryl's fear that her husband will not participate fully in raising their child, and that in the end, she'll have to take full responsibility for their baby.

When Cheryl accepts her cat, even though she thinks it's not the least bit cute, she's realizing that motherhood is more than simply a role society confers upon you—it's a relationship you forge with your baby, and this scares her. Still, Cheryl ultimately wants her baby, so much so that her greatest fear, as expressed in the dream, is losing the pregnancy altogether.

I'm having a baby, so why am I dreaming about my dog?

I remember this dream really vividly. I was in my third trimester, I had no idea what delivery would be like, and everybody wanted to know if I was having a boy or a girl. I dreamt I was in the hospital giving birth to a Mexican hairless. It was my dog, Frito, when she was a puppy. My dog, by the way, is very neurotic.

Ellen, 33, travel agent

By now you must be wondering why in this chapter called "Your Relationship with Your Baby," the dreams so far have all involved aliens and pets. The real question is, why do so many of us turn to images other than a baby to work through issues about our relationship with our baby? Because the prospect of bonding with, relating to, and being responsible for your baby can feel overwhelming, a symbol, such as an animal, can act as a buffer that allows you to explore these kinds of feelings without being threatened by them. Animals in particular can also represent things that are easy to love because they're so cute and needy.

For many of us, up until now, the experience that comes closest to motherhood is having a pet. We feed them, buy toys for them, lavish them with love and affection—they're part of the family. One of the best parts of a relationship with a pet is its simplicity. As long as you provide the basics, your pet will give you unconditional love, no matter how many times you kick it out of your room. You have to be available for your baby twenty-four hours a day, no matter what.

For Ellen, dreaming that she gives birth to her dog is comforting in its familiarity. She already has a relationship with Frito and knows how to take care of her. She knows that caring for and forming a relationship with a baby will be far more complicated and demanding. Ellen's dream reflects her feeling that her relationship with her dog is a way of practicing for her relationship with her child.

The dream is also about the people in Ellen's life prodding her for information about who her baby will be, when she already has enough anxiety about this herself. However, Ellen is less concerned about the sex of her baby than about getting through labor and delivery, and beginning motherhood. In her dream, she sidesteps the issue of the baby's sex by having neither a boy nor a girl, but having a dog instead.

Her description of Frito as being a very neurotic dog is a projection suggesting that Ellen fears she might be a neurotic mother and that the potentially overwhelming responsibility of caring for her baby might make her feel a little crazy. It also suggests that while she already knows and loves Frito, she hopes her baby won't be quite as neurotic.

What if I don't bond with my baby right away?

The dream starts just after I've given birth to a very cute, brown-and-gray-striped wild animal. It seemed from its fuzzy, tufted ears to be a lynx, and I was very comfortable with that. It crawled onto my stomach, then up to my breasts, and started nursing. That went well and also seemed perfectly normal. Then the lynx hopped off my stomach and started sniffing around the room, and once again, I was encouraged. I thought, "That's great. He's a really good animal."

Adrienne, 39, writer

Many of us have anxiety about what our first moments with our baby will be like. We may worry that we won't know how to bond right away and that we'll fail at this very first step in motherhood. There's a sense that bonding is a magical process that's very delicate, and if you so much as hold your baby the wrong way, it will be destined to a Woody Allen–length commitment on a therapist's couch. Compounding the anxiety that a single misstep can mess up our relationship with our child forever are images, which seem to be everywhere, of a glowing mother beaming at her nursing newborn just after delivery. Although we may know this isn't quite realistic, the implication is this is the way the first moments of the mother-and-baby relationship should be.

Adrienne escapes her concerns about bonding by imagining the experience to be purely instinctive—she won't have to worry because it will happen on its own. In her dream, she replaces her baby with a lynx, an animal she imagines knows instinctively how to bond and how to take care of itself. At each step of the way, she's encouraged that the little lynx knows exactly what to do. On some level, wouldn't we all like to have a baby like Adrienne's?

What if my baby doesn't like me—or worse still, what if I don't like my baby?

I dreamt I had a very mature and intense two-year-old daughter and that we had no connection to one another. With her black hair, short bangs, and intense expression, she didn't look like anyone I know. The dream took place in an area full of snowcapped mountains and fir trees. I think it was Sweden. I had a brother (in reality my only sibling is a sister) who had a very close relationship with my daughter. She seemed more comfortable talking to him than to me.

During the course of the dream, my daughter realized my so-called brother was not particularly trustworthy—he was a serial killer. She was only two, but as I said, she was very mature, and as she shared her discovery with me, we bonded over the news.

Nancy, 29, personnel recruiter

It's ironic that in some ways giving birth is the beginning of a lifelong separation process. At the same time as you're gaining a child, you're losing something that has been so completely a part of you. Realizing this can bring with it a sense of loss, even before it happens. During pregnancy, there's a unique closeness between you and your baby, both physical and emotional. Giving birth means, on some level, losing your baby as you've known it. Looking at and touching your belly, it can be difficult to imagine a time when your baby will no longer be inside you. You've been developing a special relationship unlike any you'll ever experience again, and this can be difficult to let go of.

An aspect of bonding is accepting the separation and figuring out how you can feel close to your baby once it's no longer inside you. It's a delicate emotional balancing act—you need to bond and separate at the same time. In her dream, Nancy imagines this separation as definitive; she doesn't even recognize her baby and has no idea how to relate to her, never mind bond with her. The child in her dream intimidates her, reflecting the intimidation she feels at the prospect of mothering. She worries that in some way, she won't be good enough for her baby, so much so, the child in her dream isn't the least bit interested in her. Nancy's unable to engage her or form any relationship at all. The snowcapped landscape underlines their chilling disconnection from one another. It's as if Nancy worries her real-life baby won't like her, and that perhaps she's not going to like her baby.

Like many of us, Nancy's anxieties about bonding and forming a relationship with her baby are exacerbated when she begins to imagine other people pitching in as caregivers. Whether they're baby-sitters, relatives, friends, or even her husband, she worries her baby will form an attachment to them and forget all about her.

Her brother in the dream is a composite of all these caregivers. When her daughter bonds with him and rejects her, she can't tolerate the hurt this causes her. As strange as it may seem, Nancy's relieved when she learns he's a killer. It gives her and her baby something to bond over, even if it's something as tenuous as their mutual disdain for the no-good caregiver. She can now be the trustworthy one in her daughter's eyes—the one her daughter can depend upon.

Having had a miscarriage, growing attached to this baby frightens me.

My baby plays with me from inside my stomach. I put my hand on my belly and he kicks it. Then I move my hand and he kicks it again. I love it. I wake up every morning with my hand on my stomach, ready to play.

Last week I dreamt my skin was transparent. I could look through my stomach and see his foot. It was a little, tiny foot—so cute. I had his ankle between my thumb and finger. I finally got to touch my baby.

Dierdre, 39, art historian

During pregnancy we know there's a baby inside, but looking down, all we see is stomach. Wouldn't it be comforting to have a transparent belly—a window through which you could see your unborn child? Seeing your baby could reassure you that it's okay and allow you to interact as though it were already born. With the exception of sonograms, it's hard to know what's going on in there, which can make it difficult to believe your pregnancy is real, or that there will be a real baby at the end of it. This is especially true for those of us who, like Dierdre, have experienced pregnancy loss. Often we feel the need to protect ourselves from becoming too attached to our baby for fear we might lose it.

It's difficult for Dierdre to believe she's really going to have this baby when her only other experience with pregnancy resulted in a loss. She wants to believe everything will turn out okay this time, and needs constant assurance there's a baby in there, growing and thriving. Dierdre finds comfort in this dream—not only can she see her baby through her transparent skin, she can also feel him and allow herself to connect with him in a way that's been difficult for her up until now.

It took me so long to become pregnant, I can hardly believe this baby is real.

It took me a really long time to get pregnant. I was taking fertility drugs and seeing specialists when it finally happened. I was close to my due date when I dreamt a friend and I were out to dinner and she wanted to see what my baby looked like. So I pulled up my shirt and instead of my stomach, she saw a big, round, smiling face.

Miranda, 35, TV news producer

Being treated for infertility can be an all-consuming and emotionally draining process, often punctuated with monthly disappointments. Even when you've won the battle with infertility, like pregnancy loss, it can make you doubt your body's ability to carry a pregnancy to term—no matter how many times your doctor tells you everything's okay.

Miranda had been taking fertility drugs for months and was about to begin the ordeal of in vitro fertilization, when she finally conceived. Her dream about the smiling face on her belly, like Dierdre's dream about touching her baby, assures her that her baby is in there and doing well. It also represents her happiness and relief, not just about being pregnant, but also that so far, it's gone so smoothly.

It's telling that Miranda had this dream near the end of

her pregnancy. Like many of us who have experienced the trauma of infertility or pregnancy loss, Miranda couldn't allow herself to form a relationship with her baby until just before her due date, when having a baby at last seemed like it was really going to happen. She finally feels confident enough to begin to bond with and enjoy the baby that's on its way.

Will lingering feelings about my abortion affect my relationship with my baby?

I had this dream in my third trimester. I was in a house on a hill in the middle of a forest. I was with three people, two men and a woman. They were attacking me, and I was running through the house trying to stop them. The house was dilapidated and full of antique furniture, which I kept using to put between the people and me. I thought if I just lined up the chairs between us, I'd be able to stop them. It was a huge space with a sliding door between the living room and dining room.

I managed to stop two of the attackers. I might have locked them out of the house or something. Then there was the last guy—a tall, skinny man dressed in a button-down shirt. He was coming at me, and I said to him, "Don't make me kill you like I did the other two." Then he started to walk toward me and said, "I'm going to get you because you're a murderer." He wasn't carrying a weapon, and I wasn't either. I grabbed his shirt with my right hand, and with my left hand—I'm left-handed—I grabbed his nose and tried to twist it. A long time ago, a friend told me as a self-defense thing, "If you control the nose, then you control the head; if you control the head, then you control the body."

According to my boyfriend, at this point, I started mak-

ing noise in my sleep. It sounded to him like I was saying, "Don't do this to me," and pleading with someone not to hurt me.

Julia, 33, school program coordinator

The highly-charged debate surrounding abortion can make it difficult to separate your feelings about your own experience from your politics. Even if you firmly believe in a woman's right to choose, it doesn't mean you won't experience a host of feelings—especially guilt—if you've terminated a pregnancy and are now expecting.

Having had an abortion in the past can affect your feelings during this pregnancy in ways you never imagined. Even if you were unwavering about your decision at the time, now that you're in the midst of a pregnancy you want, you may find yourself thinking about what you gave up and feeling conflicted about loving the baby you're now carrying. You probably can't help but view your relationship to pregnancy as different from before—your idea of having a baby has changed from something unwanted to something to be embraced. So it's no wonder this pregnancy can ignite new emotions about your past pregnancy and cause you to revisit feelings about it you thought you'd put behind you.

Julia's dream depicts her struggle with these issues. The maternal feelings she's developing for her baby are stirring up guilty feelings about the memory of the two abortions she had before. Guilt was never the predominant emotion she associated with her abortions, but now that she's pregnant again, these feelings have gained so much power that in her dream she calls herself a killer and a murderer. Her conflict is one shared by many women, but is extremely difficult to acknowledge—even to oneself. Julia wonders how she can love this baby and expect it to love her, when she feels like she's killed two others.

In her dream, Julia is literally being attacked by her guilty conscience. The first two attackers represent her two abortions, and the third, the baby she's now carrying. Her dream's setting, an old dilapidated house full of antiques, in other words, her old stuff, suggests Julia thinks she may collapse under the weight of the guilt and conflicting feelings her pregnancy has triggered. By stacking chairs between herself and her attackers, she's fighting to keep her past from getting in the way of the attachment she's forming with this baby. Part of her believes she'll somehow hurt this one, too, and that because of the abortions, she doesn't deserve to have a baby at all. The sliding door represents the passage from one phase of her life to another. Julia's beginning to confront her guilt so she can feel good about her pregnancy and accept herself as a mother.

Julia's attempt to gain control of the third attacker by twisting his nose is a metaphor for her struggle to maintain control over her guilt. At the same time, she's trying to control her baby, to convince it she can be a good mother, when she doesn't always feel this way about herself. Most of all, she needs her baby to believe she's going to keep it and that she's looking forward to their life together, even though it's sometimes hard for her to believe this herself.

Will I be able to love my second baby as much as I love my first?

During my second pregnancy, I dreamt my husband and I were both having babies. He wasn't pregnant, but somehow, he was able to have one. When we realized that since we were both having babies, we weren't going to have two babies but three, I became very anxious. I didn't know how we were going to manage.

Audrey, 35, caterer

Can you imagine ever loving another human being the way you love your child? After all, your child is probably the most important person in the world to you, and there may be no one else for whom you've ever had such strong feelings. But when you become pregnant a second time, you're faced with the challenge of finding it within yourself to love a new baby as much as you do your first. By developing feelings for a second child, many of us feel we're somehow taking away from the first, and wonder if there can possibly be enough of our love to go around.

Audrey has enjoyed her first year as a mother. She's been able to focus solely on her daughter, Eliza, as she's achieved all the miraculous milestones of the first year of life. When Audrey became pregnant again, she was so absorbed in caring for Eliza, and so engaged in their relationship, she could barely focus on her new pregnancy. This made her fear she'd be unable to focus on two babies at once, and worry that having a new baby would mean sacrificing the quality of the relationship she's developed with the child she already has.

Taking care of an infant has been physically and emotionally taxing for Audrey, and the added strain of this new pregnancy at times overwhelms her. Between feeding Eliza and changing her diapers while combating the morning sickness and fatigue of her first trimester, Audrey can't imagine she'll ever have the strength to give to two babies what she has been able to give to one. Dreaming about her husband having a baby without being pregnant is actually a projection of what Audrey wishes she could have for herself. But in the dream, they're each having a baby, in addition to the child they already have—as though somehow this new baby will not double the work she has cut out for her, but triple it.

I think bonding with my second child will be much easier—am I kidding myself?

I dreamt I was pregnant and that after five or six months, I went into labor and gave birth to a huge chocolate-chip cookie. At first I was surprised, but in the dream it made perfect sense. It was like, "Oh yeah, that's what happens—you give birth to cookies."

Eva, 26, homemaker

Eva's first pregnancy was unplanned; in fact, she was opposed to the idea of having a baby at all. But she decided to go through with it, and after giving birth, had a complete change of heart about motherhood. It turned out to be a joyful and defining experience for her, one she likens to realizing a dream she never even knew she had. Now that she's pregnant again, she's enjoying the experience—actually reveling in it—and looking forward to having this baby more than anything. She's been able to begin bonding with her baby without the degree of ambivalence she experienced with her first. Like a batch of cookies baking in the oven, she can hardly wait till the baby's done, which is why she dreams she has the baby so early. This time, Eva feels ready to be a mother.

Many of us enter our second pregnancy feeling we already know what it will be like. We're probably not quite as anxious or conflicted as we were during our first pregnancy, though we may revisit some of the same issues. For Eva, having a cookie—one of life's simple pleasures—instead of a baby, expresses her hope that this next phase of motherhood will be relatively easy and just as fulfilling for her. But Eva's dream also suggests that along with her joy, she worries that this new baby will complicate her life. In a strange way, it makes sense that she removes these complications by giving birth to a cookie. After all, a cookie makes no demands—its sole purpose is to be enjoyed.

Your Relationship with Your Family

Your role within your family will begin to change now that you're starting a family of your own.

I want to be close to my family, but I'm struggling to create boundaries between the family I grew up in and the one I'm starting.

I'm the first one in my family to have a child, but I'm not the oldest—I have an older brother and an older sister. I dreamt my entire family was with me in the hospital. I'd just had the baby, a boy, and I was shocked because he looked like my younger brother when he was a baby. The baby looked nothing like us. He had dark hair and eyes, just like the rest of my family. My husband and I are both very fair.

The room was barren, but there was a big party going on, and nobody was paying attention to me. My family brought a lot of food and they were yukking it up with turkey and mayonnaise. My husband was missing, the baby was crying, and I was trying to figure out what to do.

Kim, 32, accountant

Pregnancy is a time when many of us consider the meaning of family. It can bring with it the hope of becoming closer to the family we come from, yet it also marks the point where we separate from them by starting a family of our own. This can make us feel conflicted about where we really want to be in relation to our family.

If there have been times in your life when you haven't felt particularly close to your family, becoming a mother can raise your expectations and make you believe this will now change. And if you've always been close, you may struggle to create boundaries between the family you grew up with and the one you're starting.

In Kim's dream, this is played out when her entire family comes to the hospital to celebrate her baby's birth and ignores her, suggesting she finds it difficult to balance her desire to remain part of her family with her new identity as a mother. Kim associating the baby with her younger brother expresses her conflict about which family she and her baby really belong in. The baby looks like the rest of the family, but Kim doesn't, implying that while the baby fits in she's somehow an outsider.

Being the first of her siblings to have a baby confers upon Kim a position of prominence and honor within her family. But in her dream, her new status doesn't seem to make her special at all. They're having a party, and she's not included—she's left feeling like a wallflower. The food imagery relates to Kim's concerns about whether anyone will take care of her and help her with the baby. While her family is "yukking it up," no one feeds her or comforts her crying baby, expressing Kim's worry that when her family does try to help out, they'll do it in a way that satisfies them without taking her actual needs into consideration. Her husband's absence suggests she worries that he, too, won't consider her needs or share in the responsibilities of parenthood.

Kim's dream also explores how having a baby will affect her social life. She realizes that once her baby's born, it will be difficult for her to simply meet a friend for a drink or go to the movies with her husband. She imagines her old social life will be replaced by visits with her family. But in her dream, everyone in her family seems to be having a good time except her, suggesting she fears this will be a less than satisfying option.

My pregnancy has deepened my relationship with my mother in so many ways.

I dreamt I was in this very nice furniture store with my mother. It was full of reproductions of antiques. We were having a great time, and I had all the money I needed to buy whatever I chose. So I would walk down the aisle picking out things for the baby, and my mother would just say, "That's beautiful, take it."

Gail, 37, art director

It's almost impossible to go through pregnancy without having all sorts of thoughts and feelings about your mother, and being pregnant can confer a new importance on your relationship with her. As you prepare to become a mother and prepare your home for your baby, you may find yourself wanting to share more experiences with her and needing more of her emotional support—more of her time, advice, approval, and acceptance. Even if you haven't sought her guidance in a long time, she's the natural person to turn to now, since after all, she's the one who took care of you when you were a baby.

If your relationship with your mother has generally been a good one, during pregnancy it can deepen and evolve in a way that's enriching. There's the possibility for the two of you to become closer and bond over the idea of a baby coming into the family. And for the first time, your status in life is going to be the same—you'll both be mothers. You may also feel like you have a new importance in your mother's eyes because you're giving her a grandchild.

Many mother-daughter teams have an activity they enjoy doing together. For Gail and her mother, it's always been shopping. Shopping has taken on a new significance for them—it's a way to share the excitement of expecting Gail's baby. Their shared interest in creating a beautiful environment for the baby is just one of the many ways Gail's pregnancy is bringing them closer.

While this new closeness is depicted in Gail's dream by her shopping trip with her mother, buying reproductions of antiques also expresses Gail's desire to reproduce some of the idyllic childhood moments she had with her. But as Gail invites her mother to become closer, she's also setting boundaries. By being the one who picks out all the things for the baby and pays for them, she's asserting her own identity within the closer relationship they're developing. Still, what she wants most from her mother is her approval— not just for her taste in furniture, but for her ability to create a home for her baby and to be a good mother, as well.

When the baby arrives, will it be possible for my mother to help me without trying to take over?

We've been staying at my mom's house while renovating our apartment. It's a pretty big place—there are two floors. During my second trimester, I dreamt I'd given birth there and had twins. I know I'm expecting just one.

For some reason I hadn't seen them yet. I was down-

stairs and my mother was upstairs with the midwife and some other people who attended the birth. She was down the hallway, but I could see her through the stairwell. The babies were also upstairs in my old bedroom, and I was calling to her because I wanted to meet them.

I think she told me to come upstairs because the next thing I remember, one of the babies was coming down the hall. He was the size of a newborn, but was toddling down this long strip of green carpet. He was wearing a little vest, all dressed up as if he were going to private school. My mother was standing behind him, all proud. I guess she had dressed him.

Vicki, 39, textile designer

When it comes to our mother's involvement during our pregnancy and after the baby's born, there's a fine line between just enough and too much. For example, we may consider having our mother stay with us as soon as we get home from the hospital, since the idea of having someone in control, who can help take care of both of us, can be a relief. Yet we may worry she'll overstep her bounds and possibly judge our mothering skills, even at this early stage. This conflict is especially strong for Vicki. Pregnant with her family's fifth child, she realizes she needs her mother now more than ever.

It can be difficult to imagine yourself as a mother when you've always viewed your own mother as the real thing. And the idea that she may not be able to accept you in what's always been her role can make it difficult for you to accept yourself in that role, no matter how many children you have.

To Vicki, her mother is the genuine article. Even though she's already given birth to two children and is a stepmother to two more, she's always felt like less of a mother than her own mother is. When Vicki was in her own home, her role as a mother was clearly defined, and she felt more confident in herself. But staying with her mother has intensified Vicki's sense of not quite measuring up—in this household, she's no longer the mother, she's the child. This is emphasized in her dream by the twins' presence in her old room, an environment she associates with being a child. Vicki is so confused about her place within her family, she's afraid her twenty-two-month-old son, Jack, believes Grandma's house is his home, and perhaps that Grandma is really his mommy.

Vicki worries the same thing will happen with the baby she's expecting. This conflict is played out in her dream, in which she's an observer rather than a participant in the birth and mothering of her children. She gives birth to twins, one representing Jack, the other, the baby she's carrying. When Vicki discovers that one of her twins is no longer a baby, she's describing another fear—that by bringing a fifth child into the family, she's pushing Jack out of his babyhood.

In the dream, Vicki's babies, the midwife, and the attendants are upstairs with her mother, implying her mother plays a more central role in the birth than Vicki, who's downstairs, absent from the whole scene. However, abdicating her maternal role has an upside for Vicki, as it allows her mother to insulate her from the pain and difficulties of childbirth and childrearing. But in exchange, she allows her mother to take away so much that's important to her—her glory for giving birth, the satisfaction she gets from having children, and her authority as a mother.

When Vicki sees how her mother's dressed her baby, it seems to her that her mother has all the authority over her child while she has none. The prep school uniform also represents a parenting style quite different from Vicki's, suggesting that when it comes to helping with the baby, her mother will do things her own way and their opposing styles of mothering will become a source of conflict between them, as it has in the past.

My relationship with my mother is complicated, and I'm not sure what level of involvement I want from her once my baby's born.

My mom's always accidentally killing her pets. She's dropped fish down the garbage disposal, her kitten ended up in the dryer, and she even suffocated my cockatiels. Let me explain. I had three cockatiels when I was a kid. She was cooking with these new nonstick pans she bought off TV, not realizing they let off toxic fumes if you don't wash them first. Toxic to cockatiels, anyway. They started hyperventilating, then fell right off their perch, dead.

Anyway, I had a dream where my mom came to visit me. I had a basket of puppies—little itty-bitty puppies, so small you could hold them in the palm of your hand. The mother dog was there, too. She was a dachshund, but the puppies were all different breeds.

In the dream, my mom and I were petting all the puppies. Then she decided to put the smallest of the litter, the white one, in my contact lens case. I didn't see her do it, but when I opened the case, I saw tiny egg yolks, and asked, "Mom, what's this?" She said, "Oh, no, I put the puppy in there because I thought it would keep it warm." I ended up getting really mad and yelled at her. I told her to get out, and that I didn't want her anywhere near my puppies.

Laurie, 23, bartender

Even if your mother somehow fell short of the mark and disappointed you, you probably still feel a need or have a wish to connect with her at this important time. Since your relationship with your mother is unique, your issues with her—and your reactions to them—are unique as well. One daughter may perceive her mother as cold and aloof; another may regard her mother as overbearing and intrusive; and another, like Laurie, may see her mother as well-meaning but utterly incompetent. Now that you're having a baby, you may wonder how your mother's shortcomings will affect not only your relationship with her, but the way in which she'll relate to your baby, as well. You may also worry that you've inherited some of her faults, and question how they'll affect what you're destined to be like as a mother.

While Laurie's experiences are somewhat extreme, figuring out how much participation you want from your mother—and what type of participation that means—is almost always an issue, especially if you've had a lot of conflict with her. You may feel like you're in an emotional tug-of-war between wanting your mother to be there and feeling she should be, and worrying that her presence will somehow be negative—or even destructive—to you or your baby.

As far back as Laurie can remember, she felt she couldn't trust her mother, so much so that she moved out of the house when she was only fifteen. So it's no wonder she's questioning whether she can trust her in the role of grandmother to her baby. Yet Laurie, like many of us, hopes that having a baby will fix her relationship with her mother, but at the same time, she fears this may just be a fantasy.

In her dream, Laurie bonds with her mother as they pet the puppies together, and for a moment, she throws caution to the wind and trusts her. But when her mother puts the puppy in the contact lens case, Laurie's worst fears come true. Her mother inadvertently suffocates the puppy, a symbol of Laurie's baby. Laurie quickly realizes just how vulnerable the tiny puppies are, and how much they need to be protected from her well-meaning but misguided mother.

During pregnancy, the normal progression is, of course, for an egg to become a baby, but in Laurie's dream, it's the reverse—the baby becomes an egg. Laurie fears that instead of helping her baby to thrive, her mother's presence may have the opposite effect. And she knows that with her mother around, her work will be doubled—not only will she have to watch her baby, she'll have to watch her mother, too. The yolks also allude to the cockatiel incident from years before, an incident that might not have occurred had she been there to watch her mother.

Laurie's conflicts with her mother have been further exacerbated because her mother doesn't approve of her partner's race. Laurie wants her mother to accept and be happy about her baby no matter what, but she knows this is unlikely because her mother's prejudices seem set in stone. Her feelings about this are played out in her dream. When her mother chooses the white puppy out of the litter of mixed breeds to coddle and protect, the result is disastrous.

Laurie's also concerned she's doomed to become the same kind of mother to her child that her own mother was to her, since, for better or worse, she was Laurie's primary example of what a mother is. Who among us hasn't sworn we'd never repeat the mistakes our mother made with us— that we wouldn't say and do the things she said and did that drove us crazy. But as we approach motherhood, we may find ourselves uttering certain phrases or exhibiting certain behaviors that are just a bit too familiar. This is how we know that parts of her live within us—even as we strive to create our own identity as a mother.

I'm lucky to have had an amazing maternal figure in my life, and I hope I've absorbed some of her qualities.

I had a wonderful dream during an afternoon nap. In the dream I was driving, and as I drove along, everything around me began to get fuzzy and fade away. I pulled the car over to the side of the road as everything in my vision went black. I heard a voice speak softly in my ear—it was a very old voice, a wise voice. I immediately relaxed, laying my head down on the steering wheel.

This voice continued speaking to me. She said, "I am Grandmother. You are going to be all right. Everything is exactly as it should be. You must allow yourself to relax into the arms of your grandmother."

As she said this, I felt myself enveloped in the warmest, softest, most comforting embrace I've ever experienced. I laid my head on her breast and felt her arms encircle me with gentle strength. I heaved a deep sigh and felt the tears that had refused to come begin pouring down my face. She chuckled and said, "Good girl." She began singing a lullaby I recognized at the time, but can't remember now at all. It sounded like all the lullabies ever written rolled into one song. When I woke up, I felt completely calm and incredibly happy.

Renée, 34, yoga instructor

When we think of a grandmother, many of us conjure an image of a matriarch completely devoted to her family—a woman who is wise and seems to hold the deepest and most thorough knowledge about mothering. Even if your grandmother is (or was) nothing like that, you still may associate the word with that archetype.

If grandmothers are seen as ultimate mothers, Renée's grandmother seems to her the supreme mother figure. Renée's mother died when she was four, and from that point on, her father's mother became a mother to her. Grandma Bea is an extraordinary person. The wife of a minister and a gifted counselor herself, she raised five children on very little money. She's always taken in stray people and, if they were sick, nursed them back to health. At seventy-three, she founded a school, a library, and a mission in Eastern Europe, where, at seventy-eight, she continues to work with her husband a few months a year.

Since becoming a mother is such a monumental event, we may wish we could have an experience like the one Renée has in her dream, where becoming a mother is like a sanctioned rite of passage. Her dream has an almost religious quality, as if she's being ordained to be a mother. When she pulls over to the side of the road and her vision fades, she's entering a meditative state, where she can accept the presence of her grandmother, a sort of high priestess of motherhood. She whispers a few sanctioning words in Renée's ear, and sings a hymn that allows her to mourn the loss of her own mother.

Renée especially needs this approval because she questions her ability to be a mother when she hardly knew her own and her grandmother set such a high standard for the role. If, like Renée, you grew up with a maternal figure who seemed perfect, it can be daunting to now try to live up to her example—and to what you imagine are her expectations.

As we approach motherhood, many of us feel we need our mother's permission to take on the role, whether it's our actual mother or the woman who mothered us. In Renée's dream, when her grandmother embraces her and tells her everything's exactly as it should be, she gets the permission she needs. What's more, because her grandmother is such a strong maternal figure, Renée hopes she will pass her the torch and imbue her with some of her vast motherly knowledge.

Even though my adoptive mother is the only mother I've known, I've been thinking about my birth mother more than ever.

I had this recurring nightmare throughout my pregnancy. I was in the bathroom of the house I grew up in. It was like a locker room, but a large kind of homey one. I would stand in the corner of the bathroom, legs spread, holding my hands up against the wall, suffering through the excruciating pain of heavy labor. It was overwhelming—contractions that had no end, just one on top of another.

When I gave birth in the dream, it was always to a redheaded girl, which was odd, since neither my husband nor I have red hair. My mother and birth mother were both always with me in the bathroom. They would fight over the baby and physically pull at her. I'd wake up out of the dream crying or shaking, very upset.

Tamara, 23, journalist

If you were adopted, you'll probably face a number of issues about parenting that differ from those of women who were brought up by their biological parents—particularly issues about mothers and mothering. Like most women, your relationship with your mother has been, for the most part, based on the emotional connection you have with her.

She took care of you and was probably the most significant presence in your early life. As you grew up, she was probably the one with whom you shared some of your happiest moments, as well as the one with whom you had your most heated arguments. But one thing your relationship with your mother hasn't included is a biological connection. Now that you're having your own baby, you're probably discovering for the first time what it means to have this kind of bond with someone, and while the experience may be exciting, it can also be disorienting.

When the person who gave birth to you and the person who mothered you are two different people, it can be difficult to figure out how to perceive yourself as a mother. If you don't know who your birth mother is or haven't met her, you may find thoughts about her surfacing at this time—even if meeting her has never been a priority for you before. You're not necessarily longing to develop a relationship with your birth mother, but during pregnancy, it becomes important to know where you came from. You may want practical information, such as anything in your birth mother's medical history that could affect your baby, or you may be curious about who she is, what she looks like, and what kind of personality she has. These kinds of thoughts and emotions can be confusing. You may be unsure which mother to identify with, and you may feel disloyal to your adoptive mother for even thinking about your birth mother, whether you've met her or not.

Before you became pregnant, you may have had enough emotional distance to understand the possible rationales your birth mother had for giving you up. But now that you're expecting and beginning to feel a bond with your own baby, you may find yourself wondering, more than ever, how your birth mother could have let you go and rejected you so completely. You may also fear that her seeming inability to be a mother could have been passed down to you.

Tamara met her birth mother shortly before becoming pregnant. Their first meeting was a traumatic experience for Tamara. Her birth mother looked just like her, except she suffered from schizophrenia and was a drug addict living in a dilapidated, trash-strewn apartment. It was like looking in a mirror and seeing a darkly distorted reflection. Tamara was in her early twenties, and though she was married, she felt that becoming pregnant at her age would be the worst fate in the world. Yet the meeting stirred up so many emotions in Tamara, that unconsciously, it made her feel she needed to have a child of her own, despite her conscious disdain for the idea. On some level, she hoped having her own baby would make her feel more normal and more complete.

While Tamara's mother was always supportive of her desire to meet her birth mother, when she told her about the meeting and her pregnancy, her mother had a total emotional collapse. Tamara's begun thinking about her mother's infertility, and in some ways feels guilty about being pregnant. She wonders if she's even entitled to have the experience, since it was never an option for her mother. She feels there's a piece missing in their relationship; she knows she can't turn to her mother for advice about pregnancy because that would be hurtful, and because her mother has no firsthand information on the subject.

The imagery in Tamara's dream describes her feelings about her two mothers. The homey aspects depict the connection she feels to the mother who raised her, and the institutional and unfamiliar aspects highlight her lack of connection with her birth mother. She's laboring in the corner with her two mothers present, but they're not giving her any support. It's as though with two mothers, Tamara feels like she has none. For Tamara, neither woman is a complete mother, which makes her wonder if she can ever be one. Being backed into the corner is another expression of her feelings about having two mothers—she sees no way out of what feels like a no-win situation.

When Tamara pictures her mothers struggling over the redheaded baby, it describes her fantasy that both want her badly enough to actually fight over her. It also describes her feelings about being caught between the two of them; she fears that having feelings for one would seem like a betrayal of the other. Since neither Tamara nor her mothers have red hair, the redheaded baby is a metaphor for Tamara's hope that her baby will be different from the three of them, unsullied by the emotional confusion of adoption. The redheaded baby also symbolizes a new identity for Tamara, one with less emotional baggage and the possibility of a new kind of attachment—she will be this baby's mother and be biologically linked to it, too.

I'm glad my father is so enthusiastic about my pregnancy—but sometimes, I can only take so much.

My father's a born salesman—he can sell anything to anybody. I dreamt he was showing my husband and me a house. The tour began in the foyer and he showed us the living room, the family room, the dining room, and the kitchen. He was so excited to show it to me—he was unusually happy. It was an older house, full of antiques, and there was a big crowd of people there getting the same tour from my father. I was pregnant in the dream, and I liked the house, but I didn't want to buy it. I was just getting a kick out of my father being so excited.
Rachel, 37, copywriter

Fathers often see pregnancy as a club for women only. Still, your father may try to involve himself however he can so he won't be relegated to being a bystander at such an exciting time. A common way for him to do this is to try to step in and take care of you.

Your father may regard pregnancy as a more fragile state than it really is, and he may become as protective of you now as he was when you were a child. You may enjoy this new level of interest and involvement from your father, and it may be the first time in a long while that you've been able to share so much of yourself with him. But sometimes this level of involvement crosses the line and begins to feel like an intrusion.

Your father's renewed involvement in your life, coupled with his desire to take care of you, can make you feel like your relationship with him has reverted to the dynamic that existed when you were a child, except that now he doesn't wield the same authority. You may have realized that while some of your choices may disappoint your parents, as an adult you're free to set up your life as it suits you.

In Rachel's dream, her father's not trying to sell her a house so much as a lifestyle—one he believes is right for a couple with a child. The house he shows her is an old one filled with antiques, suggesting old-fashioned values, harking back to the way she was raised. Rachel grew up in a suburban home, but she and her husband plan to raise their child in the city apartment where they currently live. By showing her the old house, Rachel feels her father is judging the kind of environment she's making for her child, as well as her ability to raise it properly. Still, she's thrilled that her father is emotionally invested in her pregnancy.

In her dream, Rachel not only asserts her independence by rejecting her father's ideas about how she should live, she also questions his sincerity by referring to him as a born salesman. That there's a large crowd of people waiting for the same tour implies that on some level, she feels she's no more special than anyone else in the crowd—if she doesn't buy into the bill of goods he's trying to sell her, someone else could easily take the house, and take her place.

My father seems to treat me with more respect now that I'm having a child.

Even though I know I'm having only one baby, I dreamt I had triplets—all boys—and surprisingly, it was a very easy labor. I had all three in one shot. I was with the babies in my parents' crowded apartment in Estonia, and I was asking my father what we were going to do economically, et cetera. He was pleased I had boys—he really was not pleased when my mother had a second daughter. But he was confused that there were three. He didn't know what to do. I didn't know how to feed them, either.

Paulina, 34, office manager

As young girls, most of us saw our father as larger than life and wanted to be special in his eyes. No matter what our relationship with him was like, in some way, we wanted to please him. Even as grown women, it can seem like we're on an endless search for his approval. Pregnancy can bring with it the hope we'll finally get that approval by fulfilling the traditional female role of becoming a mother and giving him a grandchild.

Daughters are often treated differently from sons, in ways ranging from subtle to not so subtle. Take, for instance, the way they're referred to. Even as a toddler, a son is often referred to as a "little man," whereas a grown daughter may still be called a "little girl" or even a "little princess." And while a son may gain his father's approval by achieving success in his career, as women we may feel no matter what we accomplish professionally, our father defines success for us as having children.

Some fathers even subscribe to the antiquated idea that boys are more valuable than girls, though they may be unaware of it. If you know your father values boys more, it can be difficult to believe anything you do is good enough unless you actually present him with a boy.

As a young girl, Paulina sensed she didn't quite measure up in her father's eyes. She never knew why until her mother told her, years later, that her father was disappointed about having only daughters. When Paulina became pregnant and learned she was having a boy, she thought she'd found a way to finally gain his approval—by giving him a grandson. Paulina was so set on this idea that in her dream, she gives him not just one grandson, but three. It's as if she's trying to unconsciously right the wrongs of the past—if she wasn't good enough for him, maybe her son will be.

One way that fathers show they love us is by taking care of us. Each father does this in his own way, whether it's by offering advice, giving financial assistance, spending time with us, or coming over to help fix things. For those of us like Paulina, whose father hasn't always been as available as we needed him to be, we may maintain the hope or fantasy that someday this will change.

Although money was tight, Paulina's father always made sure there was enough food for the family and that their basic needs were met. But he rarely made Paulina feel special or showed her the kind of attention she wanted. When she looks to her father to take care of her babies in the dream, she's not asking him to be the actual provider—

she's asking him to show her how special she is to him and how much he loves her.

Paulina turns to her father for financial guidance and help in her dream, expressing her anxiety about supporting her baby—feelings stemming from her childhood. In addition to portraying himself, her father also represents her husband, to whom she now looks for reassurance that she won't have to relive the hardships she endured as a child. Her insecurity about her financial stability is so deeply embedded that she can't let go of it, even though she knows she now has enough money to provide amply for her baby.

In her dream, Paulina is also looking to her father for practical guidance. Like many of us, she feels overwhelmed about having a baby, and she wants him to give her the kind of fatherly advice he's never offered. She believes he should know how to help her, and how to solve the problem of taking care of three babies. But she quickly learns that even after raising two daughters, he doesn't know any more than she does and can't be there for her in the way she needs.

Now that I'm having a baby and my parents and grandparents are getting older, I'm becoming more aware of life's cyclical nature.

I haven't thought about my grandfather in a while, except that we're naming the baby after him. My grandfather, my mom's dad, whom I adored, has been dead for almost three years now. Last night I dreamt he wasn't really dead and my grandmother, whom I love more than anything, had locked him away and was trying to hide him from my mother, my two aunts, and me. When we found out he was alive, we all dyed our hair blond and curled it to disguise

*ourselves and then went searching for him. We rummaged
in and out of dressing rooms on our hunt, but I woke up before we could find him.*

Judy, 30, publicist

Choosing a name is one way we begin to bond with and
express our aspirations for our baby. When we name a child
for someone, we're honoring that person; we may even
hope our child will possess the qualities we cherish in them.
Naming a child for someone who has passed away can also
be a way of keeping that person with us.

Our relationships with our grandparents are often particularly special. These relationships are usually less complicated than those with our immediate family, since they
aren't mired in the day-to-day conflicts we have with our
parents and siblings. As a result, the love between us can be
easier to experience, which was the case with Judy and her
grandparents. Dreaming her grandfather is still alive articulates Judy's wish that he could be here to meet his name-
sake and to see her as a mother.

But her positive feelings about honoring him in this way
are undermined by her fear that she's somehow replacing
him, thereby betraying him. Although she wants her baby
to have his name and feels it's a way for her to keep his
memory alive, she knows it will also be a reminder of his
absence. What's more, Judy worries her grandmother will
feel the same way. This is played out in her dream by her
grandmother locking her grandfather away, or in other
words, locking away the pain she feels over losing him.

The prospect of naming her baby for her grandfather has
also heightened Judy's awareness of life's cyclical nature. In
her dream, a generational shift is occurring. As Judy takes
her place with her mother and aunts, her grandmother is

not included, forcing Judy to face the painful idea of her grandmother's mortality.

Becoming a mother is like joining a club in which we feel an immediate bond with its members—other pregnant women and mothers. For Judy, this club includes her mother and aunts. When she dyes and curls her hair with them, it's a female-bonding ritual that somehow solidifies her status as one of the grown-up women, a role she's become more comfortable in now that she's having her second child. Still, the dressing room imagery suggests, on some level, Judy feels she needs to put on a façade to fit the role and that as she searches for her grandfather, she's also hunting for her self-image as a mother.

I'm about to have my second baby, so why do I still act like a child around my parents?

I went to a Chinese restaurant with my parents and my brother. My brother ordered several exotic dishes for us (he makes a lot of money and often likes to take us all out in a showy manner), and there was a soup that had black stuff on the bottom. It was like tar—in fact it tasted like tar and I thought that's what it was.

After the meal, we went to the bank. I told my mother I thought there was tar in the soup and that I was worried about eating tar. She said it wasn't tar, as though I didn't know what I was talking about, but I insisted it was tar and finally convinced her there might be a problem.

I said I thought we should go to the emergency room, and she said I should ask my father. But he was busy writing deposit slips, and I was afraid of having a confrontation with him, so I just said, "Fine, if you don't care about me, I can just wait." Then I felt bad and realized I sounded childish, so

I went over to my father and just said simply, "Are you al-
most finished?"

My father said he was almost finished. I felt embarrassed
at my impatience with my mother. He said we could go to
the emergency room, but reasonably suggested we go back
to the Chinese restaurant first so we could get a sample of
the tar to take with us. I thought that was a good idea, so
we went to the restaurant, but we didn't know which soup
we had. So we had to order all the dishes we'd had before so
we could figure it out. When we got to the soup, sure
enough, it had black stuff on the bottom, but it wasn't tar,
it was a lot of little fish. I again felt ashamed that I'd made
a big deal out of nothing.

Elaine, 33, English professor

When we're with family, it's easy to slip back into patterns and behaviors established in childhood. Becoming a
mother, we may feel we shouldn't behave in this way anymore, and that we should show a level of maturity on a par
with our parents. Yet pregnancy can bring with it an almost
childlike need for special attention, and we may feel caught
between our roles as a mother and as a child.

In Elaine's family, her brother has always been the center
of attention. In her dream, the family's focused on him as he
orchestrates the dinner and picks up the tab. To compete with
her brother for her family's attention, Elaine tells them she's
sick. There's a sense she needs to do something drastic to get
their attention, since being pregnant is clearly not enough.

Elaine's family relationships easily fall into old patterns.
Even when she tries to converse with her mother on an
adult level, her mother treats her like a child, and she re-
sponds by acting like one. This is played out in her dream
when Elaine tells her mother she feels sick. Her mother

doesn't take her seriously and questions her judgment, causing Elaine to react with the childish behavior of whining and trying to make her mother feel guilty. It's as if Elaine believes this is the only way she can get her mother to meet her needs or notice her at all. Yet she pulls herself together for her father, knowing he wouldn't tolerate her tantrum, and she assumes he has more important things to do than worry about what was in her soup.

The only way Elaine feels she can get her father's attention is by being the perfect daughter. As long as she presents herself that way, she's able to feel loved in their relationship. She sees his love as completely conditional and fears that if she doesn't fulfill his expectations, he'll take it away. This fear carries over into her dream, in which she's uncomfortable letting him know there's something wrong with her. It's as if she views being sick as being less than perfect, and a sign that her baby might be imperfect, too—something she believes would be unacceptable to her father.

For those of us who have always tried to be perfect for our parents, having a baby can seem like a way of coming closer to that ideal. By becoming a mother and giving them a grandchild, we feel as if we're making them proud by fulfilling their vision for us as a woman, and this can bring with it the hope that they'll love us more than ever.

In her dream, the difficulty Elaine has talking to her father about feeling sick is also a metaphor for the discomfort she has talking to him about the more physical aspects of her pregnancy. As a girl, you were probably mortified by the idea of your father knowing about your period and hoped he'd never notice your developing body. But now, it's as though your body has taken on a life of its own, so much so that intimate details about private parts of your body seem to be freely discussed over cake and coffee.

While you may be totally comfortable about this with your mother, sharing these details with your father is another story. What's more, now that you're pregnant, it's no longer just implied that you're sexually active—to your father and everyone else, it's quite obvious you've had sex in the recent past.

At the end of her dream, Elaine discovers that the black stuff at the bottom of her soup is not tar, but tiny fish—or in other words, she's not sick, but pregnant. This points to Elaine's wish that her parents would make a big deal over her pregnancy. She's ashamed of having this wish and the behavior she resorts to in order to get their attention. But since Elaine has to be so mature in all the other parts of her life—with her husband, with her son, at work—she relishes the opportunity to act like a child again.

Instead of bringing us closer, my pregnancy seems like yet another source of competition between my sister and me.

I've had dreams about my sister. She's four years older than me and has always been the one in my family who's sucked up a lot of the oxygen with her angst. She has a high-powered job in fashion. She also married young, divorced after one year, and never remarried. I've known my husband since I was a kid. We dated for years, starting in college, and then got married.

In the most vivid of these dreams, my sister and I were in a house arguing over dinner. I don't know whose house it was—it wasn't hers, it wasn't mine, and it wasn't our mother's. The dinner was complicated, and I was dealing with the hot food. It might have been a roast chicken, and it was becoming very messy. While I rushed around the kitchen, she was just lolling about on a nearby settee. There were other people in the house and more guests were coming, though I'm not sure who they were. All I remember is I was rushing so much in the dream, I woke myself up saying, "Will you make the fucking salad already?"

Maddy, 34, financial writer

During pregnancy, as our role within our family changes, so do our relationships with our siblings. This can be especially apparent if you're the first to have a baby. Before, no matter how old you were, it was clear that you were the kids and your parents were the parents. Now that you're becoming a mother, your status is changing, but your siblings' status is remaining the same. While your siblings are most likely sharing your joy, the fact that you're having a baby and becoming a mother can unleash all sorts of issues about competition and envy.

When it comes to your relationship with your sister, the changes brought about by pregnancy are often particularly thorny and highly charged, since competition between siblings of the same sex is usually more intense. So if your sister thinks your mother cares more about you and pays you more attention, or vice versa, you can be sure that issue will be exacerbated now that you're having a baby. What's more, while there are certainly other attributes valued in the family that your sister may possess, for a daughter, the one ultimately most valued is becoming a mother.

Maddy and her sister Michelle both have successful careers, though Michelle's is more prestigious and even glamorous. And while Maddy is a bit envious of what her sister has achieved professionally, she's surpassed her in what she believes to be the more important area—family life. Another layer in their relationship is what Maddy sees as her sister's envy of her stable marriage and her pregnancy. In Maddy's eyes, Michelle, being four years older, should have had this by now. At the same time, she's upset that her sister's issues about relationships and having children have kept her from warming to the idea of Maddy having a baby. It hurts her that her sister was the last guest to show up at her shower and that she actually becomes tearful whenever Maddy's pregnancy is discussed.

On the surface, Maddy's dream simply describes the kind of scene that has played out between her and her sister since they were kids. But the argument over making dinner is not only about Michelle rarely being helpful in situations like that, it's also about the two of them struggling over who will have the glory in the family—is it the one with the prestigious career or the one having a baby?

The dream setting, an unfamiliar house, represents neutral territory. Meeting in this house implies a wish to start over, but it quickly becomes obvious the sisters have brought their issues with them. The kitchen, on the other hand, is not so neutral—it's Maddy's territory, a place where her sister seems useless. Making dinner is evocative of Maddy's pregnancy. As she rushes around dealing with the messy chicken, it evokes labor and childbirth. The dinner is complicated, as is Maddy's relationship with her sister. Maddy deals with the hot food while her sister's making the cold salad, symbolizing the cold attitude she projects about the baby, as well as the idea that she's green with envy.

I hope having a baby will bring my siblings and me closer together.

I'm in my third trimester, and I just had a very disturbing dream. I dreamt my husband and I lived in this big two-

story house, and I wanted to bring the baby downstairs for a while. I gathered all the items the baby might need, so I wouldn't have to make a trip back upstairs. My brother, whom I don't see very often, was in this dream and was helping me do this.

So I carried everything downstairs, and my husband said, "Do you have everything?" And I said, "I feel like I've forgotten something." Of course, I'd forgotten the baby. So I ran back up the stairs, to where my brother was, and we couldn't find the baby anywhere.

We searched and searched frantically, and no baby. Suddenly, my brother screamed, "Oh, no!" He told me he'd set the baby outside the window on the roof for a minute to get some air. I screamed and ran to the window, and there was my baby, rolling around on this small eave of a roof, inches from falling off. I snatched him up, heart pounding. My brother apologized for forgetting the baby. Then I woke up.

Sonia, 22, purchasing agent

The joy and pride you feel about having a baby often have a ripple effect within your family. For your siblings, this can mean looking forward to watching you become a parent and to becoming an aunt or an uncle themselves. But feelings about life-changing events are more complicated than that. The very fact that you're about to become a mother can touch on all kinds of sore spots your siblings may have, causing them to experience mixed emotions. Because of this, you may feel you're not getting the reaction from your brother or sister you hoped for. Instead of unabashed joy, you may sense undercurrents of their own issues about pregnancy and parenthood, as well as all of your shifting roles.

Many of us hope our siblings will want to become more involved with us during our pregnancy and especially after the baby's born, and that the baby will somehow bring us closer, no matter what our relationships have been up until now. Having a baby offers the opportunity to reexperience the sense of camaraderie we shared when we played together as children. And as adults, we probably want our siblings to share our experience of becoming a parent and to develop a special relationship with our child.

As children, Sonia and her younger brother were so inseparable they were known as Frick and Frack. When she told him she was pregnant, she expected him to be happy for her, but instead, he seemed uncomfortable with idea. She attributes this to the two of them being in different stages of their lives. Despite an age difference of only two years, Sonia is married and starting a family while her brother is single and relatively carefree. It seems to Sonia he can't relate to what she's going through or be fully supportive of it. Dreaming about her brother being involved with her and the baby describes her wish that this wasn't the case.

Like many of us, Sonia has her own criteria for what she expects from a her brother as an uncle, and she questions whether or not he can ever come close to filling the role. This is played out in her dream when she entrusts the baby to him and he leaves it on the roof, inches from falling off. Sonia has had trouble trusting her brother in the past, and this incident expresses her difficulty trusting him in any context, let alone with her baby.

On another level, Sonia's dream about her brother leaving her baby is a projection of her own issues about becoming a mother. Sonia's mother left when she and her brother were very young. With this as her role model, she worries she's in danger of not being a good enough mother. The baby also represents Sonia and her experience of what it felt like when she and her brother were left, as well as her fear that she could do something like that to her baby.

Having a baby makes me feel like I've lost my mother all over again.

This dream took place in a sun-filled room with a bed that had a canopy. Everything in the room was white and really bright from the sun. It looked like heaven. I was sitting on the bed with my mother. She looked exactly like she did before she died, except she was radiantly healthy. She was still very thin, but had a beaming smile and a full head of salt-and-pepper hair.

I was four or five months pregnant at the time, but in the dream I looked like I was due. My mother loved being in that room with me. She smiled and laughed and talked about the baby. I told her how much I love my husband, spilled all my happiness and my fears. We were having the mother-daughter conversation I'd always wished we'd been able to have.

She held my belly, and I couldn't take my eyes off her hands—she had these amazing, long fingers. "This is wonderful," she said. "The little girl is going to be great." At the end of the dream, she was in the delivery room, standing by the bed while I was giving birth. It was strange. She was immediately given the baby, and I could only see my child wrapped in a blanket in her arms. I never saw my baby's face.

Valerie, 25, bookkeeper

During your pregnancy, memories of your mother at different stages of your life are more present, and you may find that thoughts of her are with you all the time as you contemplate yourself in the role that's always been hers. If your mother has died, these thoughts and memories can cause you to experience her loss all over again, and you may feel like you're missing out on an important part of your pregnancy—sharing it with her.

The joy of having a baby can be diminished by the knowledge you'll have to go through it without your mother, and that she and the baby will never know each other. It can be painful to watch other women share their pregnancies with their mothers when this isn't an option for you—especially since you may feel you need her in ways you never have before, or at least haven't in a long time.

Valerie married and started trying to become pregnant shortly after her mother died from cancer. They had been close, but they'd never had the opportunity to share such important moments as Valerie's becoming a wife, and now a mother. She sorely felt her mother's absence during her wedding preparations and when she walked down the aisle. Now that she's having a baby, she misses her mother more than ever. Valerie's dream is a way to reconnect with her mother and share these milestones, as well as a wish that she could be with her now.

If your mother has passed away, at times you may still feel a need for her approval. For Valerie, this means dreaming about her mother smiling and holding her pregnant belly, an image that allows her to experience the approval for her marriage and pregnancy her mother is not around to give her, but that she still longs for. At the end of the dream, the faceless baby in her mother's arms expresses Valerie's hope that her baby will somehow be connected to her mother, and that in some way, it will be as though her mother is still with her.

It makes me sad that my baby and my father will never know each other.

In my first trimester, I had a lot of vivid dreams about my father. He would be sick in the hospital like he was in the last part of his life, except he was sort of mobile and animated. When he was really sick in the hospital, he was definitely immobile. In the dream I told him, "Daddy, I'm pregnant," and watched him walk around the room in a weird, grotesque way that scared the hell out of me. I cried when he answered, "I know you're pregnant, but I'm dying."

Barbara, 34, food importer

Knowing that your baby and your father will never meet and that your father will never see you as a mother can add a new dimension to your grief over his loss. You may experience painful feelings even more acutely than before because now you don't just want him to be there for you, you want him to be there for your child.

Barbara's father died six months before she became pregnant, and she's having a hard time feeling joy over expecting a baby while she's still mourning him. All at once, she's been confronted with the dichotomies of life and death, ultimate joy and deepest sadness, and finds it almost too much to bear. In some ways, she doesn't even feel entitled to experience happiness about her pregnancy, and when she does, she usually feels guilty about it.

Barbara's frequent dreams about her father express a desire to connect with him—to tell him about this exciting time in her life and how much she needs him. But when she tells him she's pregnant in the dream, his response is more about sadness than joy. He dismisses her and reminds her this can't possibly be a happy time, setting the tone for her confused feelings.

Picturing her father as animated implies that by having a baby, Barbara wishes she could somehow bring him back to life. But his actual movements in the dream are grotesque and frightening. They force her to relive his death and face the idea that he can't be there for her anymore, and that her child will never know this man who was so instrumental in shaping who she is.

I'm worried about how my other children will feel, once there's a new baby in the house.

During my second pregnancy, I dreamt that a bunch of exotic birds had escaped from a pet store. These were big, colorful macaws, much more glamorous than my little Buster, the parakeet I owned at the time. I was on a mission to help these birds. I was trying to either capture or recage them.

Angela, 35, realtor

Those of us who already have children usually experience some anxiety about the prospect of introducing a new baby into the family. We may have carefully planned for another child and think another sibling would be great for our children. Yet we can still have a nagging fear about the effect the new baby will have on our family and how the dynamic will change. Just telling your children you're pregnant and explaining what that means can be an unenviable task. If your children are young, you may be especially worried about them feeling jealous and displaced by the new baby. You may also wonder how you're going to give this baby the attention it needs and deserves without making the other children feel left out.

Angela's situation is a bit different. She has three children—two preteens and one young teenager. But this baby will be the first child she and her husband are having together; the others are from their previous marriages. She worries the other children will somehow think the baby is more special to her and her husband, since it's the only one that will be connected to both of them right from the start. Angela even worries they may go so far as to ignore the baby and not accept it as part of the family.

Angela feels guilty that she's so focused on her pregnancy. When she attempts to recage the exotic birds in her dream, it's as though she's trying to convince her children to stick around and remain part of the family. Helping the birds, symbols of her children, is a way to keep them from feeling rejected. She fears if she doesn't do the right thing for them, she'll somehow lose their love. The act of capturing and recaging the birds also represents her need to control her children and to protect her new baby. She fears that just as the macaws could gang up on the defenseless parakeet, her older children could gang up on the baby she fears they'll perceive as an intruder.

Your Relationship with Your Friends and Colleagues

As your life changes, so does your perception of your friends and colleagues, as does their perception of you.

I worry some of my friendships will fall by the wayside once I become a mother.

I was walking down the side of a deserted country highway surrounded by friends from different times in my life—friends I met traveling, friends from high school, friends from work. They don't all know each other, and I haven't seen some of them in years, but they're all people I have very positive, close associations with. In the dream we were very content just to be together.

As we ambled along the highway, I started to wonder why no one noticed I was pregnant. So finally I lifted my shirt to reveal my new, round belly. Everybody was very happy for me.

The group gravitated to an underground road, which led to an underground theater. One of my friends, who actually has never been pregnant, gave me all kinds of maternity clothes.

Jocelyn, 28, environmental lawyer

During pregnancy we begin to feel a shift in our relationships with our friends, and know this shift will probably become even more dramatic once our baby's born. We
may find ourselves developing closer bonds with our
friends who are also expecting or who are already parents.
And while our friends without children may share our excitement, there can be a sense of a growing gulf between us.
Whereas at one time we may have felt they completely understood us, now that we're having a baby, they can no
longer truly relate to what we're going through.

For Jocelyn, dreaming about bringing together people
from her past is a way of helping her move into the next
phase of her life. She associates these people with times
when she felt freer, and while her dream contains a longing
for what was, there's also the sense that she's trying to integrate her old friendships with her new life as a mother.

Jocelyn's dream includes two powerful metaphors for
travel—a highway and an underground road, symbolizing
her journey to her new life as a mother. Walking along these
roads with her friends underscores her hope that she can
take them with her on this journey. The underground road
marks the path to her unconscious, and the theater holds its
contents. Her unconscious contains her questions and anxieties about how combining her identities as a mother and
as a friend will play out on the stage of her life.

Like many of us, Jocelyn fears once she becomes a
mother, she'll be socially isolated, and may lose some
friendships entirely. Dreaming that a friend who had never
been pregnant is giving her maternity clothes suggests that
she's hoping all her friends, including the ones who don't
have children, are going continue to be a part of her life and
that they will accept and embrace her in her new role. Beyond that, having all her friends react so positively to her

pregnancy validates her sense of herself as a mother and the idea that these relationships can continue to thrive. This makes her feel better about the changes happening in her life and relieved that she'll still be able to maintain the relationships she'd formed before her pregnancy.

Mothering seems to come so naturally to my friends, but I worry it won't for me.

My dream is related to something that happened about five years ago, before I even thought about becoming pregnant. I wanted to adopt a kitten from a shelter, but I was in the process of moving and thought it was the wrong time. My friend Amy convinced me I should go ahead and do it anyway, and promised to take care of it until I was settled in. A week later, she told me she was absolutely in love with the kitten and wanted to keep it, which was fine with me, since I was doing a lot of traveling for my job.

When I was about three months pregnant, I had this dream. I'd had the baby and I was really busy, so I immediately gave it to Amy to take care of. I didn't even know its sex. A year later she calls and asks if I want my baby back. We meet in the elevator of my building and I ask her whether I had a boy or a girl. She tells me I had a boy, but I'm a bit confused because the baby she hands me is wearing a dress. "It's the only clothes I had," she explains. In real life, Amy's an attorney and has twin baby girls.

Beth, 33, pharmaceutical sales

During pregnancy, it's only natural to compare ourselves to our friends who are already mothers. It's a way of making sure we'll meet the standard for parenting set by our peers. It's also a way of learning from them. As we begin to take an active interest in the minutiae of parenting, we become keen observers of what everyone else is doing. We notice how and what our friends feed their babies, what brand of stroller or diaper they're using, and whether or not they endorse the use of pacifiers.

Many of us know someone like Amy, a powerful figure who seems to be able to take care of everything and everyone—a supermom who effortlessly manages a busy career without missing a beat in her children's lives. It's easy to be in awe of such a woman and wonder if it will be possible to ever measure up. But just as you may not want to follow precisely in your mother's footsteps, as you develop a sense of yourself as a mother, you may not want to do this with the friends you look up to, either.

Over the years, Beth has depended upon Amy for all sorts of things, and when she thinks about the responsibility of caring for her baby, she can't imagine doing it without the support system Amy represents. When Beth had this dream she was unsure how she would incorporate a baby into her busy life, or even if she was emotionally ready to be a mother. In her dream, she turns to Amy, hoping she'll once again come to her rescue, and Amy does so by taking the baby. This articulates Beth's issues about how much she can—and should—rely on a friend, or anyone else for that matter, who has more mothering experience than she does. She worries that relying too much on others will mean forfeiting her own experience of being a mother.

At the end of her dream, when Beth discovers that for the past year her friend has been dressing her son like a girl, she realizes that even though her friend seems like the perfect mother, she's not—at least not for Beth's baby. Beth is beginning to understand she'll be the best mother her baby can have, even though she doesn't yet feel fully prepared.

Sometimes it seems as if there's an unspoken contest between my pregnant friends and me.

I dreamt I was at the hospital giving birth to a boy. At first he was a little baby with straight, brown hair, and he looked just like my husband and me. But very quickly he became a three-year-old blond. It was very confusing. I remember feeling disappointed that I missed his infancy. I was also disappointed that I had a boy. I don't know what my baby's sex is, but I'm hoping for a girl.

At one point in the dream, I'm with my best friend, Jamie. She just had a baby five months ago, and all she talks about is how wonderful it is to take care of an infant. In the dream, we're out taking a walk. Her baby is a tiny girl, and I mean really tiny—six inches long. My baby, on the other hand, is a big boy who's very energetic and a little unruly.

Meredith, 37, research scientist

When it comes to taking major steps in life, we often take our cues from our friends. Whether it involves career, marriage, or having children, it can take one person within a circle of friends to open the door for the rest and give them the courage to follow. But seeing a friend move ahead to the next level and attain a new status can also spark competitive feelings and make us wonder if it's time for us to take that next step, too.

Competition is a normal part of friendship. As children, we compete with our friends in just about every way—we compete to see who can run the fastest, get the best grades, or snag the cutest guy. This doesn't really change much once we become adults, except that as our relationships grow more complex, the competitive aspects can become less obvious. Since we may feel our need to compete is somehow petty, particularly in personal relationships, it can be difficult to acknowledge this aspect of our nature. However, competition can be a positive force that motivates us to set and reach goals.

Pregnancy can seem like yet another arena for competition between you and some of your friends. But there's a difference between competing and simply comparing, though there's often a fine line between the two. You may find yourself comparing every detail of your experience with your pregnant friends, which can feed every anxiety you have about your pregnancy. For instance, if you have morning sickness, you may race to the phone to find out if you're experiencing it the same way a friend did, or if you don't feel your baby move as much as a friend feels hers, it can be cause for alarm.

As you compare yourself to the expectant mothers in your circle, comparison can easily cross over into competition. You may begin to notice and truly care about such issues as who's gaining the most weight, whose husband is most attentive, whose job offers the best maternity package, and who's still making it to the gym. Your perception of how you measure up to others in these respects can affect your self-esteem. Sometimes, it can make you feel better about yourself; at other times, it can leave you feeling envious of your friends.

When Meredith compares herself to her friend Jamie, who seems to be having the perfect mothering experience, she can't imagine things working out so smoothly for her. For five months, Meredith has listened to Jamie talk of nothing but the joys of caring for an infant. This has made her anxious about how her own experience will measure up and, in some ways, has set the stage for a mothering competition between the two of them.

This competition is played out in Meredith's dream, in

which she must endure watching Jamie mother a miniature baby girl, who, with her doll-like qualities, seems so easy to manage. Meredith, despite her wish for a girl, has a boy in the dream. Not only is her child the wrong sex, he doesn't even remain a baby more than a few moments before becoming an unruly three-year-old. It seems to Meredith that Jamie has all the luck—she gets to mother an infant girl and doesn't even have to work that hard at it, while Meredith misses out on the joys that Jamie's been bragging about. Instead of getting to mother a baby, she skips right to the challenge of caring for an active child.

Some of my coworkers treat my pregnancy as an invitation to discuss details about my life I'd rather keep private.

I dreamt I went into labor at the office. I work in telemarketing, and we're all in an open space on one big floor. In my dream, I was in the kitchen taking my break when my water broke and I went into labor. I wasn't in any pain, so I walked over to this hospital, which was on the same floor as my office and was owned by my company.

One of my colleagues, Natalie, came with me. We're friendly, but I wouldn't want to have her present at the birth. Next, I was lying on a bed, a normal bed, and there were doctors all around. I told Natalie not to let them give me any drugs. But they must have given me something because when I pushed and the baby came out, I didn't feel anything except the sensation of warm water. The baby was a tiny boy wrapped in a blanket.

I took him back to the office. There are four women at work who I can't stand, and they, along with everyone else, were trying to touch my baby. I flipped out and told them,

"Don't touch my baby—I don't know where your hands have been!" Delia, my best friend from work, was also there. She wanted to know if the baby was okay, since he was nine weeks early and weighed just four and a half pounds. I realized that was why I didn't feel him being born. But he looked really good, and I was holding him and he didn't even cry. Then I walked through a beaded curtain, and that was the end of the dream.

Rita, 24, telemarketer

Work relationships are frequently an awkward blend of the professional and the personal that varies from one colleague to another. The people you work with are not strangers, but they're not necessarily your friends, either. Although you probably spend more time with these people than you do with anyone else, even your husband or your family, you don't necessarily want these relationships to cross the boundaries you've set. But once your colleagues know you're pregnant, those boundaries begin to crumble as they become privy to details about your life you wouldn't necessarily choose to disclose, imposing an enforced intimacy of sorts.

Colleagues often regard pregnancy as an invitation for closeness, which can feel intrusive on many levels. While sharing your pregnancy with them can help humanize the workplace, it can also make you feel like an important part of your life is being trivialized. For instance, your pregnancy may become fodder for water cooler gossip, coworkers may reach out and touch your belly uninvited, and you may be bombarded with the same questions over and over again. "When's the baby due? What are you having?" and "Are you planning to come back to work?" can be tiresome inquiries to respond to time and again. While it would seem ungracious to snub these people who are showing interest in your life, you may wonder if their interest is genuine or just a way to engage in small talk.

Rita's relationships with her coworkers range from a select few she considers close friends to those she flat-out detests. With the majority of her coworkers, however, she's cordial, but these relationships don't extend into her personal life. Before Rita became pregnant, she was able to choose with which colleagues she would share details of her life and to what degree. But now that she's visibly pregnant, she's constantly barraged with all kinds of personal questions, comments, and unsolicited advice, often from people who previously barely said good morning to her.

Rita's feeling of being intruded upon is so great that in her dream she actually delivers the baby at work and has no choice over who's by her side. She seems powerless to control the circumstances surrounding the birth. The baby arrives prematurely and at work—the last place she would want this to happen—with people she feels she can't trust and don't truly care about her. She even believes she was given drugs against her will, despite her pleas to her coworker to protect her from this very thing. When she returns to work with her baby, her colleagues touch him without her consent, as they've been touching her belly all along in her waking hours.

Rita's dream is a way of clarifying how she feels about her various work relationships—whom she can trust and be intimate with and whom she would prefer to keep at arm's length. When her best friend, Delia, tells her it was the baby's size that kept her from feeling the birth, her presence is comforting, symbolizing the type of person Rita wants with her for the baby's birth and beyond.

When Rita leaves through the beaded curtain at the end of the dream, it's as though she's trying to escape to a private place. But the curtain is only a beaded one, implying she feels she can put up only the flimsiest of partitions between her professional and private lives.

SECTION THREE

FEARS

No matter how much you know about pregnancy and motherhood, so much of what your own experience will be like remains shrouded in mystery, especially if this is your first baby. And since pregnancy takes you into unknown territory from which there's no turning back and brings with it such monumental physical and emotional change, it's only natural for all sorts of fears to surface.

The most common fears we face during pregnancy concern labor and delivery, our baby's health and survival, the idea of failing at being a mother, and the thought of losing a substantial amount of our freedom. Each of us experiences these fears differently and to varying degrees, but to some extent, we all have them. As uncomfortable as it may make us to confront our fears, exploring and acknowledging them is the best way to begin working though them.

Fears about Labor and Delivery

No matter how prepared you are, the prospect of experiencing the pain and all the unknowns of labor and delivery is still frightening.

The closer I get to my due date, the more anxious I become about labor and delivery.

Last night I dreamt I delivered my own baby. I was in my home, and I could practically hear my own voice talking me through it, "Pull the shoulder down this way. Turn it. Ease it out. Gently, gently." I'm supposed to have a boy, but in my dream, I gave birth to a girl who was healthy, but already a toddler.

Nola, 33, natural foods store owner

You're about to become a mother, and you couldn't be more thrilled. As you prepare for your baby and share your excitement with family and friends, you can't wait to hold your newborn in your arms. But beneath these pleasant thoughts lurks the realization that in order to get to motherhood, there's no escaping the pain of labor and delivery. The mysteries it contains paired with the knowledge that pregnancy has its own built-in deadline are enough to make any woman's anxiety level go through the roof. It can feel as if your pregnancy is a force unto itself, and like the tail wagging the dog, it's in control of you, rather than the other way around. The closer you get to your due date, the stronger this feeling becomes.

One of the scariest aspects of labor and delivery is that you can't predict when and where it will happen, and you're powerless as you wait for your body to signal it's time. You may fear your water will break while you're stuck with strangers in an unfamiliar place, unable to reach your partner quickly enough. Panic at the idea of being at the whim of contractions that will overtake your body. Worry that you'll behave in a way that's out of control, screaming and blurting out things you wouldn't normally say.

Nola takes control of her delivery the only place she can—her dreams. If she can't control when and where she'll go into labor, or how she'll react to the pain, then at least she can attempt to allay her fears about these things. As she delivers her baby on her own, she calmly talks herself through the process. No one is present to help her through any aspect of her delivery—she acts as her own labor coach and doctor rolled into one. By taking charge of the birth, she's supporting herself in a way she fears no one else can or will, expressing her concern that the people she's depending upon won't be there for her, at least in the ways she wants.

But Nola's sense that she indeed lacks control becomes apparent when she gives birth to a girl who's already a toddler instead of the baby boy she's supposed to have. The toddler also symbolizes the lack of control she fears she'll face as a mother. Nola knows that while labor and delivery will mark the end of her pregnancy, it will also be the beginning of her new life, and that from then on, she'll have to give up the level of control she once had.

In some ways, learning the details of labor and delivery has given me even more to be afraid of.

I dreamt I was in bed with my husband and labor just started. I could feel that the baby was in the transverse position. His head was on the right side of my stomach and his feet were on the left. He wasn't head-down like he was supposed to be. My contractions were really bad—I was writhing in pain. I thought there was no way I could get through this and I tried to wake my husband, but he wouldn't budge. I woke up in a totally tangled mess of sheets.
                                  Melinda, 29, guidance counselor

You've probably read countless books and articles on childbirth, attended classes and seen films on the subject, and spoken with all sorts of people about the experience. You know the process of labor and delivery is the most natural thing in the world and that countless women have gone through it. But no matter how much you know, the prospect of something the size of a small watermelon emerging from your body can make you want to turn back the clock to just before you got pregnant and reconsider the whole thing.

Perhaps the most frightening thing about of labor is that no matter how extensively you've prepared for it, it still contains so many unknowns. You know contractions signal its beginning, yet if this is your first child, it's impossible to know what contractions feel like. You can't predict whether your labor will take three hours or twenty-three, and there's no way to anticipate just how much pain you'll be in.

Educating yourself about pregnancy is both essential and empowering, but the irony is, as is often the case, the more you know, the more there is to feel anxious about. Learning about things that could go wrong can unleash your imagination to the possibility of these things happening to you, and make you wonder about other dangers you haven't even heard of yet. Melinda, for example, learned in her childbirth education class about the positions a baby could be in and then dreamt her baby was in the transverse position, describing her fear that this could happen to her and that she'd need a C-section. Her fear that she'll never get through the pain of labor is only compounded when she's unable to awaken her husband and get his support, making her feel she must bear the pain alone.

Having gone through a difficult delivery, I'm frightened about what this one will be like.

I had two dreams about the baby's head coming out. In one, the head was shaped like a bicycle helmet, an impossible shape, similar to the head of the creature in the movie Alien. *I was giving birth to this baby and I thought, "Oh, my God, how am I ever going to get this thing out of me?" In the end, everything was fine and the baby was healthy, only its head was this weird shape. In the other dream, I'm giving birth and I'm scared because the baby's head is very, very big.*

Magda, 39, chiropractor

Just as every pregnancy is different, so is every labor. Even those of us who have given birth before can have fears about the next one. Magda was expecting her third child when she had this dream. Her first delivery went smoothly, but during the second one she suffered a vaginal tear that took a long time to heal. Although the experience was extremely painful, Magda and the baby were both okay. More than anything, the experience was emotionally traumatic for her, since it veered from her expectation of what delivery should be like, based on her first time.

Throughout this pregnancy Magda has been trying not to think about the tearing, but it would be almost impossible for her not to. It's understandable that Magda has these fears, knowing that she's facing another delivery where the possibility exists that this—or something else totally unforeseen—can happen.

Magda's fears are expressed in her dream by her baby's helmet-shaped head, which makes delivery seem nearly impossible. The odd-shaped head also describes Magda's concern about whether the baby will be normal. Giving birth in her dream to a healthy baby comforts and reassures her that her baby will be okay, and that even though she had a difficult delivery before, this time she'll make it through unscathed.

I worry I won't be able to have the kind of delivery I've been hoping for.

I dreamt my husband and I were going on vacation. But this wasn't just any vacation—we were going on a moon shot. I knew the purpose of the trip was some kind of medical test for me. The dream began with us in the middle of a Byzantine cluster of corridors that were supposed to lead to a ladder—the kind you would see at NASA—that would take us up to the capsule.

These corridors were very crowded and noisy. My husband was navigating us through the throngs of people, but something happened. I lost sight of him and turned the wrong way.

I ended up channeled into a medical office that turned out to be an exhibit of extreme surgeries—patients in blue plastic chairs and on metal tables, some with huge tumors being removed from their necks. I thought the doctors were live and the patients were wax models. Meanwhile, I'm thinking, "Where the hell is my husband? Where's the moon shot?"

When I reached the end of the medical horrors exhibit, there was a man at a desk. I told him I was lost and asked him to direct me to the moon shot. He ignored me and continued shuffling papers. I knew that he knew how to guide me, but he insisted on taking his own sweet time. I saw another woman get his attention and got so riled by his rude behavior, I reached into my purse, took out the cell phone my husband gave me for Christmas, and called him. He was relieved to hear from me, but pissed off that I got lost.

Ariel, 38, tax attorney

Even before becoming pregnant, you may have considered what kind of delivery you'd like to have. By now, your feelings and opinions about where and how you want to give birth are probably pretty clear, whether you're planning to have your baby at home or at a birthing center with a midwife, or in a hospital under the care of an obstetrician. But no matter how formulated your opinion, you may still wonder if you've made the right choice and if your delivery will go the way you've planned.

Ariel has chosen to have her baby with midwives at a birthing center for a number of reasons. She's never felt comfortable with the medical establishment, and what's more, believes childbirth is a natural process that shouldn't require a hospital setting. In fact, the only hospital visit Ariel made during her pregnancy was for genetic counseling. The counselors tried to convince her that because of her age, she should have an amnio. When she opted against it, they didn't easily take no for an answer.

Even though Ariel ultimately did not have the amnio, the incident left her with the nagging feeling that if she had taken the counselors' advice, she would feel more secure about the health of her baby. It also left her anxious that her delivery experience will somehow deviate from the one she's been planning. Perhaps she'll be manipulated into having some kind of procedure or medication, or something else she doesn't want.

Ariel's dream provides an apt metaphor for labor and delivery. Giving birth can be likened to going on a moon shot, in which we leave the familiar behind to visit a strange, unknown world; the capsule is like the womb and waiting for takeoff is like anticipating labor. Ariel knows the purpose of her trip is medical tests, expressing her concern that the medical establishment will somehow interfere with her having the kind of birth she wants. As she navigates the corridors, she becomes disoriented and goes the wrong way. This brings her face-to-face with medical horrors, evoking her belief that going the traditional medical route is the wrong way for her. That she can't quite find the moon shot implies, while she's committed to having a natural birth, she has some ambivalence about her choice and about the prospect of going through labor and delivery at all.

Ariel witnesses medical horrors—extreme surgeries and patients with tumors—suggesting her worst fears about giving birth and about the well-being of her baby. What's more, the doctors with their wax patients represent what Ariel perceives to be the dehumanizing effect of the doctor-patient relationship. The wax patients also symbolize her difficulty conceptualizing she'll soon have a real baby. The man at the desk represents her belief that hospitals are impersonal, as well as her fear that no matter where she gives birth, she won't get the support she needs. Losing her husband suggests Ariel even fears she'll be abandoned to go through labor and delivery alone. But the cell phone is a symbol of their connection and as it was his gift to her, a symbol of a more significant gift, the pregnancy.

Sometimes I wish my husband could be the one to give birth instead of me.

I dreamt I went into labor. I was carrying the baby, but somehow, my husband was going to have the baby. When my contractions started to get a little more painful, he started having contractions, too.

Next, we were in the bedroom. He had a pregnant belly and I had to lift his scrotum to catch the baby. Every time I would go to pull the baby out, it would get in the way or fall. I kept thinking, "This is such a stupid piece of anatomy."

Finally, the baby came and I caught her. I cut the cord. Then it was my turn. I had to nurse her, because he wasn't going to. Then she turned into a cat and had big fangs.

Francine, 37, art dealer

Over the course of your relationship with your partner, you've probably suffered negotiations over your division of labor worthy of a NATO summit, concluding with agreements such as you taking out the trash while he walks the dog. But no matter how equitable your relationship, when it comes to pregnancy, fair or not, there's no question about who'll be carrying the heavier load.

Even if you're surrounded by a supportive partner, family, and friends, you're the one who has to deal firsthand with the forty weeks of pregnancy, which you know will culminate with the inevitable pain of labor and delivery. Like Francine, you might fantasize about how great it would be if your partner—or anyone for that matter—could share your burden.

Francine's dream addresses more than just her fear about the actual pain she knows she'll experience. When she describes her husband's scrotum as a "stupid piece of anatomy," it's actually a projection of her doubts about her own anatomy. She feels her pregnant body is cumbersome and worries it's incapable of withstanding the rigors of labor and delivery, or that it will in some way fail her.

Even though in her dream Francine is able to avoid childbirth, her husband immediately hands over responsibility for their newborn to her. Since he won't feed her, she must. When the baby transforms into a fanged cat just as she's about to nurse her, it expresses Francine's knowledge that childbirth will involve pain and that no matter what she does to manage it, she cannot escape it altogether.

I can't wait to finally have my baby; still, I wish I could put off labor as long as possible.

After my friend gave birth and had a simple time of it, I had this dream. I was in the waiting room at my doctor's office, sitting quietly. At the time, I thought I was going in for a checkup. My sister was with me, not my husband. She has one daughter whom I'm very close with. Someone started encouraging me to go into the delivery room—I think it was my sister—and I thought, "Shit, I better get in there."

Denise, 40, video director

Labor and delivery mark the end and the beginning of two distinct chapters in your life. Although you're probably excited to start your new life, you will undoubtedly miss aspects of what you're leaving behind. This might sound like a line from every high school commencement speech ever written, but when it comes to giving birth, the sentiment rings true. It's the moment you change from a pregnant woman with your baby inside you to a mother holding your baby in your arms. Like a high school senior who longs to cling to those final carefree days, in some ways, you, too, may want to postpone the inevitable.

The closer you get to labor and delivery, the more real the idea becomes that ready or not, you'll soon be a mother. Even with all the discomforts of pregnancy, in many ways, it's easier to be pregnant than to be the mother of a newborn. At least while you're pregnant, you're still your own person, able to come and go as you please without the round-the-clock responsibility a baby brings. What can be the most daunting realization of all is that while the days of your pregnancy are numbered, motherhood lasts forever.

Even if you can't wait to have your baby, you may be aware that giving birth brings with it a sense of loss. For many months, your pregnancy has been a very real part of you, both physically and emotionally, and in some ways, you'll miss it when it's gone. You may, for instance, miss the presence of the pregnant belly you've grown accustomed to. You may also realize that after giving birth, your baby will never be as close to you ever again. And you may know a lot of the attention you've received as a pregnant woman will soon go to your baby.

Denise hopes that, like her friend, she'll have a relatively easy time with her delivery and with her transition from pregnant woman to new mother. Her husband's absence suggests she takes more comfort from the presence of an experienced mother, like her sister, who's been through this before, than from her husband, who's as clueless as she is. That she has to be encouraged to show up to deliver her baby implies not only that she wants to postpone the pain of labor and delivery, but also that she's not quite ready to plunge into her new life as a mother.

Fears about Your Baby's Health and Survival

Until your baby is safe in your arms, it's almost impossible not to worry about something going wrong.

My doctor tell me everything's fine, but I can't help worrying that something might be wrong with my baby.

I dreamt my daughter was born with ten fingers on each hand. She was stretching them out, grasping at the air. I was shocked. I kept saying, "Oh, my God!" and counting her fingers. When the doctor saw her, he said, "Oh, my!" He had a mask on his face. I remember being so pissed off at him.

Kara, 25, paralegal

Just after hearing her baby's first cry, the archetypal question for a new mother to ask is, "Does my baby have all its fingers and toes?" Kara's dream expresses the fear of getting the undesired response to that question, as well as the fear we all have at some time during pregnancy, that something might be wrong with our baby.

As you go through pregnancy and invest yourself in it both physically and emotionally, it's normal to want reassurances along the way that you'll have a healthy, thriving baby. But no matter how well it's going, you may still fear something going wrong. These fears can occur at any point during your pregnancy. You may experience them early on before you have tangible evidence that everything's okay, whether it comes from fetal movement, sonograms, or other prenatal tests. Or your fears may set in closer to your due date; as you're able to more clearly imagine your baby, you're able to imagine more clearly things that could go wrong with it. And the more attached you become to your baby, the higher your stake becomes in its health and survival.

Fears about what could go wrong in your pregnancy can be intensified if you're experiencing any medical problems or have had them in the past, especially if you've had a pregnancy loss. But other things can factor in, as well. Perhaps you had difficulty conceiving, or your pregnancy is considered to be high-risk. Your fears can even be fueled by stories your mother told you about troubles she had during pregnancy.

These fears can also stem from a sense of guilt about having contributed to putting your baby at risk, no matter how unlikely the reality of this may be. You may worry that years of bad habits—or even the cocktail you had before you knew you were pregnant—have compromised your ability to have a healthy baby. Guilty feelings about past events, ranging from abortions to the idea that you waited too long to get pregnant, can make you believe you don't deserve a healthy baby, or any baby at all. You may even feel guilty about things in your past that are totally unrelated to pregnancy but make you feel undeserving of good things happening to you.

With the medical problems I've been having during my pregnancy, it's hard for me to believe everything will turn out all right.

I had the same dream over and over when I was pregnant, and had it again the day I brought my baby home. I dreamt he was a perfectly shaped newborn and that we were in a pool in our bathing suits, playing underwater. He was swimming and I was following him from behind without touching him. Every few moments, he would turn around and look at me with this gleeful little smile on his face.

When we reached the deep end, the expression on his face changed to a look of horror. It was as if he was trying to say, "Oh, my God, I'm in so much trouble!" I wanted desperately to help him, but couldn't because I was now stuck in a lamb's-wool winter coat and was sinking. I tried to shed the coat, but I couldn't get it undone because its buttons were the size of Coke cans and far too big for the buttonholes.

As I sank deeper, the water became darker and I completely lost sight of my son. Each time I had this dream, I would wake up crying and drenched in sweat.

Kelly, 37, nutritionist

One of the most frightening aspects of pregnancy is the idea that without warning, anything can happen at any time. This lack of control can make you feel helpless. Even if you've had a successful pregnancy before, you can still feel as if you're waiting for the worst to happen.

Kelly's first pregnancy was trouble-free, and she gave birth to a healthy baby. But this time, from the moment she found out she was pregnant, she's faced one medical problem after another. This made it difficult for her to believe she'd have a healthy baby, and what's more, helpless to do anything about it.

Kelly's dream illustrates her feelings of helplessness. The water imagery evokes amniotic fluid and the idea that she's trying to rescue the baby in her belly. She thinks everything's all right, but it turns out not to be. As she swims along behind her baby, watching over him, it's an idyllic scene between mother and child. But as they enter the pool's deep end, without warning the events take a disastrous turn. She tries to save her son and realizes she's trapped by a heavy coat, describing her sense that she's sinking and can't keep her head above water. Every time she surfaces, another problem threatens to overwhelm or drown her.

I worry that if something were to go wrong with my pregnancy, I'd be powerless to stop it.

During my first pregnancy, I dreamt my unborn baby slipped out of the womb and into my leg. I could actually see him bulging out from the side of my thigh. I tried to hike him back up into my torso. It was like pulling on panty hose, or a tight pair of jeans. Finally, after much gyrating, I maneuvered him back into the proper place.

Janet, 25, teacher's aide

Sometimes it's hard to believe your body can seemingly defy gravity and hold your baby securely inside you. If this is your first pregnancy, the entire experience is new and foreign, and you have no way to gauge if the baby is where it belongs. At times, you may even wonder if it's in danger of somehow slipping away.

Janet's feelings about the unfamiliar things happening in her body are expressed in her dream when her baby falls out of her uterus. The falling baby is a metaphor for her fear of losing her pregnancy, as well as her fear that she'll be unable to prevent this from happening. Her ability to maneuver the baby back into the womb describes her fantasy that if something were to go wrong with her pregnancy, she'd have the power to control the outcome and make everything right.

It would be so comforting if I could see what's really going on inside me.

Do you remember Silly Putty, the claylike stuff you play with? You can make things with it and stretch it, and it never dries. That way you can keep using it over and over again. But what's really cool about Silly Putty is you can press it onto a comic book, lift it up, and see the image perfectly, right on the clay.

I dreamt somebody stretched Silly Putty across my pregnant stomach. When they peeled it off, I could see a full color portrait of my twins. The pictures were so meticulously drawn they almost looked like bas-relief. I could make out that one of my babies was a boy.

Ashley, 27, executive assistant

Since it's almost impossible to relate to someone you've never seen—who's not even born yet—it's only natural to create mental pictures of your baby and even vignettes about what your life together will be like. If your doctor has put you on bed rest, you have plenty of time for these kinds of musings, but you also have ample time to mull over the risks that put you there. So as your relationship with your baby develops and intensifies, your fears about losing your baby can intensify, too.

Ashley is spending the last trimester of her twin pregnancy on bed rest due to premature labor. She needs reassurance that she won't have any more contractions and that she'll have two healthy babies. In her dream, she gets reassurance from a low-tech sonogram that uses Silly Putty instead of electronic equipment. It creates an image of her babies that's much more detailed and realistic than the fuzzy image actually found in sonogram pictures. What's more, if this image indicates something's wrong, she can fix it—the Silly Putty gives her the ability to sculpt and shape her babies, allowing her to control the outcome of her pregnancy.

It took me so long to conceive, I can't bear the thought of losing this pregnancy.

I had this dream three times. Without having to go through labor, I take the baby out to see what she's like. Each time she's clean and perfect, like a little doll. But it's always too early for her to be out in the world and I can't put her back in.

Morgan, 29, film editor

For many of us, sonograms just aren't enough. We want more tangible proof that our baby is thriving and need to know exactly what's going on inside us. Fertility problems can make this need even more intense. If you've been through fertility treatments, you may recall how easy it was to obsess over every detail of your cycle and the all-encompassing anxiety you went through each month about whether or not you were pregnant. So if you've experienced infertility, it can be hard for you to believe you're really pregnant, and all the obsessing you went through while trying to conceive may now be redirected to the pregnancy itself. At first, you may doubt there's a baby at all and want constant proof it's really there. And as your pregnancy progresses you may find yourself obsessively worrying about the baby's health.

For Morgan, becoming pregnant was an arduous process involving fertility drugs and scheduled sex. There were times she thought she'd never conceive, and even now that she's in her third trimester, sometimes she can hardly believe she's pregnant. This is played out in her dream when she takes her baby out to confirm that it actually exists and that it's okay. Her need to see her baby is so strong, she can't keep herself from taking it out, even though it's too early for the baby to survive in the world, and she can't put it back in where it would be safe. This expresses her fear that if she worries too much, her stress will somehow harm her baby, no matter how unlikely it is for this to happen.

After losing my last pregnancy, I need constant reassurance that this one's okay.

I dreamt I came home from work and told my husband I figured out this trick I could do. I could take the baby out of me and pop it back in. I showed my husband how to do it. The first time I showed him, it was a boy. Then I did it again and the baby's arms turned into lobster claws. I remember laughing and thinking it was a joke, but he was very nervous.

Regina, 32, business development

Pregnancy loss is almost always traumatic and brings with it a special kind of sadness. Although you never had the opportunity to get to know your baby, it was part of you and your hopes for your future. When you become pregnant again, the excitement you feel is often accompanied by memories of the sadness you felt at the end of your last pregnancy, as well as the fear you'll lose this one, too.

Up until now, Regina's only experience with pregnancy has been loss, and it's difficult for her to imagine that this one will end any other way. Because of this, she dreams of a way to monitor her baby—by popping it out, making sure it's okay, and then popping it back in to safety. Her need for this kind of system highlights her fears about not being able to control the outcome of her pregnancy, as well as her wish that she could have somehow prevented the miscarriage she experienced last time.

When Regina laughs after seeing her baby's lobster claws, she's trying to minimize her fears about something going wrong. It's hard for Regina to tolerate all the anxiety she feels about this pregnancy, so in her dream she lets her husband do the worrying.

Now that I'm pregnant again, I'm haunted by the memory of the miscarriage I had before.

I dreamt I had another miscarriage. I went to the bathroom and was bleeding and bleeding. But at the same time as I was sitting on the toilet, I was telling myself this is just a dream.

Anita, 39, travel agent

If you've miscarried, it may have been difficult for you to come to terms with your feelings about it. Now that you're pregnant again, some feelings you thought you already resolved can return with even more strength than they had before. You may be surprised at how anxious you feel during this pregnancy and find yourself looking for signs that the pregnancy is still there and doing well, whether it's hoping for morning sickness, running to the bathroom to make sure there's no blood, or going to the doctor three times a week to hear the baby's heartbeat.

Realistic dreams like Anita's are pure manifestations of the kind of panic that sets in when one imagines losing a pregnancy. Her dream is so frightening and her memories of her miscarriage so visceral, she has to tell herself she's not really losing her baby, and that it's just a dream.

I have no real reason to worry, so why am I so afraid of losing my baby?

I've had a lot of dreams about preterm labor. In one I was lying down looking at my belly and it was transparent. I could see my baby and he didn't look right. He was tiny, the size of a pea, and in a clear amniotic sac, like a baby would be at six weeks' gestation.

The baby popped out of my belly button. This happened several times. I don't know if it was more than one baby, or the same baby at different stages, because at first it was the size of a pea, then the size of a quarter and more developed. Finally, it was the size of a baseball and looked like a little, pink Casper the Ghost.

He looked up and waved at me with his little hand. He was holding his umbilical cord as if he was smoking it, and he was smiling at me like, "This is good stuff."

There was a tear in the amniotic sac, and the fluid was draining out. I thought, "Oh, no." So I went to my refrigerator where I had amniotic fluid in a squeeze bottle. I tried to warm it by holding the bottle between my legs. Then I put the baby and the sac in a Ziploc bag, filled it with fluid, and put it back in through my belly button. Then everything was fine.

Shannon, 23, customer service

You're enjoying your pregnancy. Your doctor says you're doing well. You're feeling pretty good, sometimes better than good. Yet every now and then, you're stricken with the fear that something will go wrong. You know there's probably no concrete cause for your concern, but you also know pregnancy is a mysterious process, and even if all the indicators say everything's fine, there are no guarantees.

Although Shannon's having a healthy pregnancy and has no actual reason to worry, she finds herself worrying anyway. She's focusing on preterm labor because she's heard about it from a couple of friends, but any of us can latch on to any of the myriad fears associated with pregnancy.

Shannon's dream is about her fear of either having her baby prematurely or losing it altogether. The portrayal of her baby as a ghost is a symbol of this. While the friendly waving ghost is a hopeful image, being a ghost also suggests he's no longer alive.

Seeing the different stages of development expresses Shannon's wish she could somehow see her baby growing and progressing. In her dream, being more aware of the nitty-gritty of her pregnancy enables her to take care of and control any problems that arise. When the fluid leaks and her baby's in jeopardy, she's amazingly prepared to prevent a disastrous situation. It's as though, on some level, she knows even though she has all these fears, chances are everything will turn out okay.

I worry that my age will in some way compromise my pregnancy.

I was in a tropical forest where there was a war going on. I could hear the deafening sound of gunfire all around me, and there were all these soldiers trying to rush me through the danger. I didn't look pregnant, but I carried an egg that contained the baby. The egg was completely covered with chocolate.

The soldiers made me wade through a lake, and as the water rose higher and higher and I reached its deeper sections, I worried the chocolate might melt and the baby might die. The egg was about eight inches high, but I decided to swallow it whole, so it would be inside me where it's safe.

Eliza, 38, film producer

If you're over thirty-five, you may have been alarmed to see your doctor jot on your chart Advanced Maternal Age. "How can this be?" you're thinking, "I just finished paying off my student loans. And I still have acne!" But unjust as it may seem, in reproductive terms the medical establishment—and perhaps your mother—considers a woman in her midthirties to be fast approaching her twilight years.

Whatever your reasons were for waiting to have a baby, now that you're pregnant, you may worry that your body won't be up to the task of maintaining a healthy pregnancy. Eliza knew postponing pregnancy was the right choice for her, yet she can't help worrying and feeling guilty that by waiting, she may have inadvertently put her baby at risk. Although she knows plenty of women her age and older who've had healthy babies, she still fears she'll be the exception.

In Eliza's dream, she allays her fear that her body will be unable to sustain pregnancy by dispensing with it altogether. Instead, she carries an egg outside her body as she walks through the war zone—a symbol of the risks she perceives pregnancy to entail as well as her lingering doubts about her choice to wait. Having an egg also enables Eliza to keep her pregnancy at arm's length, a way to keep herself from growing too attached to the baby she fears she'll lose. The danger makes her realize that despite her misgivings about her body, it's the safest place for her baby, and so in order to protect it, she swallows the egg and allows herself to trust her body and embrace her pregnancy.

Fears about Not Being a Good Mother

Even if you feel competent in other areas of your life, when it comes to motherhood, you may fear you'll somehow fall short of the mark.

I'm afraid I won't have the faintest idea how to take care of my baby.

I had a dream where my baby came out and was talking to me. I was holding him, and he was instructing me on how to take care of him. He said with this TV announcer voice, "I'm hungry and you have to care for me. Now you have to comfort me, so rub my arm." In the dream, I was thinking, this is not normal.

Rose, 26, market researcher

Wouldn't it be great if babies could tell us exactly what they need, and we weren't left to decipher the meanings of all their whimpers and cries? It would certainly make us a lot less anxious about the idea of taking care of our baby once it arrives. Instead, many of us feel we should some-how instinctively know what their needs are and how to take care of them, yet fear we won't have a clue.

As your pregnancy progresses, chances are that at times you've felt uneasy or even overwhelmed at the thought of caring for a baby, and you may worry about your ability to be a good mother. You may fear that you don't have the right instincts—that you won't be able to protect your baby or know how to feed it properly. You may also feel unprepared to care for it, physically or emotionally. While this is particularly true for first-time mothers, those of us who already have children may also worry about our ability to be a good mother once there's another child to take care of.

Rose's dream expresses the fantasy of having a baby with the ability to articulate its needs, eliminating the need for any guesswork on its mother's part. Rose's baby is born giving her very specific instructions, practically micromanaging his care. He has the voice of a TV announcer, a quintessential communicator. Her fantasy stems from her fear that she won't know how to comfort or care for her baby. In her dream, she doesn't have to know how, because he tells her exactly what to do and how to do it—all she has to do is follow his instructions.

Even though my baby isn't here yet, I feel like I'm already a bad mother.

I had this dream right before I got the results of my amnio. I dreamt I was in a living room cluttered with knick-knacks. Every surface was crammed with elaborate little glass and ceramic objects, what seemed like hundreds of them, that were small enough to swallow.

I was following a toddler around, who was clearly pre-verbal. He was cruising from one piece of furniture to another. I was alarmed because he kept touching the objects and trying to put them in his mouth. I'd barely have taken one away from him, when he'd reach for another and quickly slip it into his little mouth.

> *Finally, after what must have been at least six or seven at-*
> *tempts to stop him, he turned to me and said very clearly and*
> *impatiently, "I'm hungry!" I remember feeling surprised*
> *and amused. But I also felt like a poor mother for not reading*
> *my child's body language accurately. The next day I found*
> *out I was having a healthy baby, thanked the heavens, and re-*
> *solved to at least be more conscious about my prenatal diet.*
>
> Jessica, 36, cellist

A mother's instinct to protect her baby doesn't simply appear when it's born. During pregnancy, many of us feel we'd go to any length to make sure our baby's okay, and make many changes in how we take care of ourselves to create as safe an environment for our baby as possible. Slipping up—even to the slightest degree—can make us feel guilty and that we're not being a good enough mother, even at this early stage.

Awaiting our amnio results, most of us experience anxiety as we hope to be reassured about our baby's well-being, yet fear we won't be. Jessica's anxiety is exacerbated by her sense that she hasn't taken good enough care of herself during pregnancy. This has also brought up fears about her ability to take care of her baby once it's born. She wonders how she'll control what her baby puts in its mouth when she feels she hasn't been able to control what she puts in her own. Jessica fears that once her baby arrives, she won't be able to figure out its needs or how to respond to them, and that she won't be able to protect her baby from the infinite types of harm that exist.

In her dream, she tries to do the right thing but is ineffectual. To protect her son, she attempts to take the dangerous objects away from him, but at the same time, she's misreading his cues. By attempting to eat the knickknacks, he's trying to tell her he's hungry. When he finally speaks, it's as if he was forced to learn for survival. If he left his fate to his mother's instincts and her ability to understand him, he would surely perish. It's as though he's accusing Jessica of having neglected his needs, making her feel as though she's already failing as a mother. Since babies often put things in their mouths for reasons entirely unrelated to hunger, Jessica's setting an unrealistic standard for herself as a mother by assuming she should have instinctively known what her baby was really trying to tell her.

How will I ever be able to protect my baby from all the dangers in the world?

I had a dream about two animals—one was doglike with long nails and strong teeth; the other was a vulnerable, white poodle puppy. At first they both seemed like babies to me. Then the one that was just kind of doglike went after the poodle. It seemed rabid, and it picked the puppy up with its teeth. I screamed at the animal, "Drop that puppy!" and lifted the injured dog into my arms. I held the puppy like a baby and saw that its side had been punctured by the other animal's nails. When I looked at my hand, it was covered with the puppy's blood.

Jeanne, 28, optometrist

As you prepare to become a mother, the world can seem like a menacing place where danger lurks at every turn, whether these dangers are within your home, your neighborhood, or the world at large. Things you used to accept, or were at least able to filter from your conscious mind, resonate more deeply now that you know you'll soon be responsible for keeping someone completely helpless out of harm's way. News stories depicting acts of violence, crime, and environmental crises now take on new meaning. And for the first time, you're probably paying attention to a whole different set of issues that are of particular interest to parents, whether it's car-seat recalls or bad meat in school lunches.

Like many of us, sometimes Jeanne is overwhelmed by the idea that her baby's life is so fragile and that there's so much she needs to protect it from—both during pregnancy and after it's born. She fears she won't be able to protect her baby, or to even recognize danger when it's present.

In her dream, an animal she perceives to be a baby becomes a rabid dog, embodying the dangers she feels she must shield her defenseless baby from. The puppy, on the other hand, represents her baby. She practices being a mother as she rescues it from the other dog's jaws and cradles it in her arms. The two dogs also suggest the different ways Jeanne imagines her baby—her fantasy of a cuddly, vulnerable baby as well as her fear of one that's unmanageable and impossible to relate to.

I've prepared everything I can possibly think of for the baby—so why do I still feel so unprepared?

One night I dreamt the baby arrived as a miniature version of a full-grown man. I think he might even have been smoking, just like the baby with the cigar in the Bugs Bunny cartoons. He was very annoyed at me for not having his room prepared for him and not at all shy about expressing his feelings. I think all his complaining woke me up.

Casey, 33, boutique owner

Part of the fun of preparing for a baby is picking out all the furniture, equipment, and cute little things it will need. However, the amount of stuff you're made to feel you must have for a baby can be overwhelming, and as you sift through an avalanche of articles, advertisements, and advice, that fun can quickly be replaced with a headache. And the irony is that your newborn will care about its layette, furniture, and wallpaper pattern least of anyone.

There can be a sense that if you prepare your home for your baby physically, then you'll somehow be prepared for it emotionally. The accoutrements of a baby help reinforce the idea that there'll soon be an actual baby living there. So much is involved in having a baby that's out of our control that controlling the things we can, such as the baby's environment, can have a calming effect. Since much of this need to prepare comes from an emotional place, even if you do manage to organize everything to the last detail before your baby arrives, you still may not feel quite ready.

In Casey's dream, her baby appears as a fully grown man who's annoyed with her for her lack of preparedness, making her feel as if he's judging her and that she's not a good enough mother for him. He's an adult in the dream, and a domineering one at that, putting her in the seemingly absurd position of having to answer to him. However, the real problem isn't that Casey hasn't prepared her baby's room—it's that she doesn't feel fully prepared herself.

Will relying on others when my baby's born mean I'm incapable of taking care of my own baby?

I'm supposed to be getting a baby nurse. I dreamt she couldn't come and sent someone else in her place. The re-

placement was horrible, and she looked just like my aunt's nurse, who was also horrible. All I wanted was to fire her, but I didn't know how. I was sure she sensed my antipathy, so to get back at me—this nurse was really malicious—she dropped the baby in front of all of us. My parents, my husband, my brother, and I were all screaming, and I think the baby was hurt. I was so freaked out by the dream that I called the woman I hired and made her promise that when the time came, she'd be there.

Celia, 26, jewelry designer

As your due date approaches and you imagine finally being home with your new baby, the prospect of caring for someone so tiny and helpless can seem staggering. Many of us will rely on the help of someone experienced at that time, whether it's our mother or mother-in-law, sister, or a baby nurse. While their presence can help reassure us, the idea that we might need someone to take over the responsibility of caring for our newborn—not to mention the disparity between our skills—can make us feel inadequate. It can also make us feel we lack the innate knowledge of how to take care of our own baby and even doubt we have the emotional wherewithal to be a mother.

Celia's anxieties about becoming a mother are embodied in her dream by the presence of the baby nurse. The wrong nurse showing up symbolizes her fear of being unprepared for the baby's arrival and for motherhood itself. But it's her need for the nurse to be there in the first place that expresses her anxiety that she'll have no idea how to take care of a baby on her own. This makes her feel that she'll not only be a bad mother, but that she's also somehow unworthy to be a mother at all.

Along with her self-doubt, Celia's dream describes her

fear that if she depends upon others, they may let her down. Her husband and family's presence in the dream expresses her hope that they'll be able to help her. Yet when the nurse drops the baby, the very people she depends upon are as helpless as she is. Celia realizes if something were to happen to the baby while in someone else's care, it will be her fault, since she believes the baby is ultimately her responsibility. The nurse is also a projection of Celia's sense that she's the incompetent one, capable of dropping the baby or making equally disastrous mistakes.

I think I use good judgment in most areas of my life, but I'm afraid I won't when it comes to being a mother.

I dreamt I'd had my daughter—I knew I was having a girl. I put her in my knapsack like a papoose, and because it was raining, I covered her in cellophane and put a poncho over her.

I was walking on a country road, then down an embankment and through a thick wooded area. When I came out, there was a giant mall in front of me. It was cold and damp outside, so I went in. I was in a store looking at all these neat nautical instruments, when I remembered my daughter was in my knapsack, under the poncho and cellophane. I thought I was the most horrible mother.

I started to peel off the cellophane, and this well-dressed couple said, "Oh, my God, she's having an arrhythmia." They took out a stethoscope, listened to the baby's heart, and checked her all over. It was a typical newborn examination and they were very official—they had rubber gloves and a doctor's bag.

The woman said my daughter wasn't doing so well and needed to be checked out, and that they were affiliated with

a hospital down the road. They said, "Leave the baby with
us. We're going to run some tests—just go home and wait."
    I went to my friend's house where I was staying. She asked
me where my daughter was, and I realized that she'd been kid-
napped.

Georgia, 37, personal assistant

Even if you feel competent in most areas of your life and
think you usually exercise good judgment, when contemplating the countless decisions involved in caring for a
newborn, you may fear you won't be able to rely upon your
own judgment at all. And if you already tend to feel insecure about your judgment, the responsibility of making
these decisions can be that much more difficult.

In her dream, Georgia keeps questioning her mothering
instincts and her ability to make the right decisions involving her baby's care. When she loses confidence in herself,
her reaction is to hand her authority over to others she believes to be more capable than she is. Her actions in her
dream come from a logical place, at least in the world of
dream logic; when it rains, she covers her baby with a poncho, but she covers her with cellophane, too. Georgia's
judgment, though well intentioned, misses the mark. When
she realizes she's left her baby under cellophane, she
doubts her ability to be a good mother. The nautical instruments she looks at represent her longing for an inner com-
pass to guide her and give her direction as a mother.

When the well-dressed couple rushes to her daughter's
aid, Georgia perceives they are accusing her of having
harmed her baby. They present themselves as authority figures just when Georgia's failings as a mother have made
her feel particularly vulnerable, which makes her trust
them more than her own instincts. It takes her friend to ask

her where her daughter is to make her realize that she has once again exercised poor judgment.

I'm afraid I won't be capable of nursing my baby.

I had one dream where I actually saw the baby—a beautiful little girl wrapped in a pink blanket—and she had a full set of teeth. We were lying on my bed, and we were both very sleepy. She was crying and I was trying to breast-feed her, but since I was so tired, I was having some trouble at it. When I looked over at the baby to see how she was doing, she had milk all over her mouth and was grinning at me with this big, toothy smile.

Jayne, 28, hairdresser

We've all seen new mothers deftly nursing their babies, making it seem so incredibly easy, and we hope that feeding our newborn will go just as smoothly. Feeding is, after all, the most basic mothering skill—a child's very survival depends upon it. But you may fear that when the time comes, you won't know how to feed your baby, and that if you somehow fail at this, you won't be able to get anything right.

You may have already decided whether you'll breast-feed or bottle-feed, and if you haven't, it's probably something you've at least thought about. Choosing between the breast and the bottle can be an emotionally charged process, since there are so many factors and influences to consider, some of which may be conflicting. While you've probably formed your own opinion on the subject, the advice of your doctor or childbirth educator, the opinions of your family and friends, and what you've read can all play a role in your choice. Still, whatever decision you make can bring with it its own set of anxieties.

If you've decided to bottle-feed your baby with the current trend being to nurse, you may still have mixed feelings about your decision, even if you're certain it's the right choice for you. And if you've chosen to breast-feed, you may not be able to picture yourself nursing. It can be hard to imagine a time when your milk will come in if you've had no evidence of it so far, and you may wonder if you'll produce enough, or any at all. You may also worry you won't be able to get the hang of nursing, or that it might be unbearably painful.

In Jayne's dream, she initially has a great deal of anxiety surrounding breast-feeding, particularly fear of the pain it might entail, as illustrated by her baby's full set of teeth. Despite her fears, it turns out nursing comes naturally to both Jayne and her baby, which makes the prospect of nursing her real baby a lot less scary.

Why do I keep dreaming that I can't find my baby?

One of the most common scenarios in pregnancy dreams is forgetting, misplacing, or in some way getting separated from our baby. This type of dream—the realization of a mother's worst fear—usually stems from anxiety about whether we'll be a competent mother. Since in many of these dreams our own negligence causes the crisis, they express our fear that we might somehow allow this to happen in real life, and perhaps don't even deserve to have a baby at all. There are probably as many variations of this dream as there are women who have them. The dreams below are just a few:

Throughout my first pregnancy, I had recurring dreams about being off at a party having a good old time and sud-

denly thinking, "Oh, my God—we forgot the baby!" The dream happened at all different kinds of parties with all different friends, but it was always the same feeling and I always woke up totally terrified. We were a couple used to doing couple things, and I had no clue about being responsible for a baby.

Patsy, 25, teacher

I dreamt the baby was in his carriage, and I was strolling with him on a street full of stores. I stopped to look in the window of a shoe store. After months of wearing sneakers and flats, I couldn't take my eyes off all the pretty high-heeled mules. When I turned to continue walking, the carriage—and my baby—were gone.

Meryl, 35, interior decorator

Early in my pregnancy I had a recurring dream that I couldn't find the baby. I'd be in the apartment looking for him behind the furniture and under the bed. Then I'd be looking for my fiancé, and I wouldn't be able to find either of them. I'd get so scared, I'd wake up in a sweat.

Carla, 28, financial analyst

During my first pregnancy, I dreamt I was on the subway with my baby. When it was our stop, the doors opened and I pushed the stroller onto the platform. But before I could get off the train, the doors closed, separating me from my baby. As I pounded on the doors, the train began to quickly move, and all I could see was the stroller all alone on the platform, getting smaller and smaller in the distance.

Freddie, 32, actress

Fears about Loss of Freedom

As you prepare to take on the responsibilities of motherhood, it can be frightening to realize just how many restrictions will soon be placed upon you.

I'm afraid that when my baby's born, I'll lose whatever freedom I still have.

I had this dream in three scenes.

Scene 1: My husband, Philip, and I were living in New Jersey in a small, isolated house near a railroad track at the end of the line. I was involved with the FBI investigating trains and spies and deliveries. My job was to monitor activity connected with the train line, to gather information. We weren't married yet, and I've never lived in the country, but it was my house and Philip was living with me.

Scene 2: Same house in New Jersey, but it was also my apartment in Manhattan. I was with my previous boyfriend, David, and Philip was out of town. That it was my apartment is how I morally reconciled being with my ex in what could have been Philip's house.

Philip was traveling for business, and David was staying over for several days at a time. We would just hang out and I would cook dinner, and we were definitely sexually involved. In this scene I really felt like I did when I was in

that relationship. Also, this time I was on assignment for
the Mossad because David's Jewish.
    Scene 3: Still in the house. David's gone. Philip's back.
And I'm thinking, "Wow, I pulled that off."

Helen, 38, artist

Whether you've just found out you're pregnant or are
well into your third trimester, you know your days of unencumbered freedom are numbered. Although you're probably looking forward to your baby's arrival, you're also
realizing you may never again have the kind of freedom
you're accustomed to. Even leaving the house for something as simple as a quart of orange juice will be impossible
without first considering the baby. It can be frightening to
think of all the restrictions that will soon be placed upon
you, so it's only normal to fantasize about times in your life
when you felt free.

You probably think that once you're a mother, your focus
should be entirely on your baby and your own needs should
take a backseat—or for that matter, no seat at all. It's what
you may believe society expects of you and perhaps what
you expect of yourself. Yet you may be reluctant to accept
this level of selflessness, and this can make you feel guilty.

As in many of our dreams, the house in Helen's dream is
a representation of herself, and its isolated location symbolizes her fear of becoming isolated once she's a mother. She
describes the house and the apartment as hers, not her husband's. Yet, the house still holds some connection to her
husband, since it's in New Jersey, where he lived when they
first met. The apartment is hers only; it's where the affair
with her ex-boyfriend David occurs, and it represents the
part of herself that longs for freedom.

Like many of us, Helen associates her freedom with her

single days. The train line symbolizes her fear that, once she becomes a mother, it will be the "end of the line" for the freedom she's known. This makes her long for a time when she had fewer responsibilities and life was more carefree, represented in her dream by her liaison with David. Their affair represents her desire for pleasure and freedom, while her jobs with the FBI and the Mossad, as well as the allusion to spies, represent her conscience, which makes her feel guilty for not playing by the rules.

The idea that the deliveries need to be monitored suggests the possibility of a dangerous situation—the danger of Helen losing her freedom once her baby is delivered. By testing how far she can take the affair, she's trying to figure out how much freedom she'll be able to "pull off," implying that for a mother, freedom is not to be openly desired, but is something only to be enjoyed surreptitiously.

Will I be able to have any social life at all when I become a mother?

I've had dreams where I'd go out with friends and be like, "Oh, wait! I have to go home to my baby." Usually I've left the baby on the bed and there are people in the house, but I haven't asked anyone to care for the baby while I'm out. I always spend the rest of the dream struggling to get back to my baby. That struggle of getting home is awful because I never seem to get there. I'll see myself walking in the right direction and then I end up at another party thinking, "What am I doing! I'm supposed to be going home." In these dreams, when I do get home, someone has always taken care of the baby and it's fine. I think it's about me realizing I can't just go out and leave.

Terry, 31, computer analyst

As we contemplate motherhood, it's easy to become nostalgic for the social life we'll have to leave behind and to even begin to feel claustrophobic as we realize how restricted our lives will become. We know for the time being we'll have to trade in our evening bags for diaper bags, and that our primary concern will be making sure our baby is taken care of, no matter where we are or what we're doing.

For those of us who are single mothers, there can be an added dimension of fear attached to the idea of a severely curtailed social life. Not only do we worry about having less fun, we also worry that finding a romantic relationship will be as likely as winning the lottery. What's more, without a partner at home, we may wonder where we'll find adult company, not to mention someone to help share the responsibilities of the baby so we can have some time to ourselves.

Terry's used to going out whenever she wants and spending a lot of time with her friends. As a single mother she knows this will have to change, but she really doesn't want it to. In her dream, neglecting to ask anyone to take care of her baby suggests it's difficult for her to accept that there will soon be a baby who will restrict her freedom.

Terry's dream is like a Cinderella story in which she's off at the ball, perhaps looking for Prince Charming. When she remembers the baby, it's as if the clock's struck midnight and she knows she'd better get home. Her struggle to get there represents the part of her that doesn't want the responsibility of a baby, but that she keeps trying to get home suggests she realizes that no matter how she feels, caring for her baby will be her responsibility.

Now that I'm becoming a mother, I feel like I shouldn't even think about my own needs anymore.

I was in my gym clothes working out, either on a bike or in spin class, and I gave birth to a beautiful baby girl. Then three weeks go by and I'm back at the gym wearing short-shorts and a jog bra and everyone's telling me I look great. At first I just bask in all the attention, but then I panic because I can't remember what I did with my baby. I look everywhere for her and can't find her.

So I go home and ask my husband if he's seen her, and he says he put her in the vegetable drawer to keep fresh. I restrain my fury as I imagine my baby girl cold and stiff like a head of lettuce and ask what he's fed her. To my horror, he says, "I gave her whatever I was eating."

Gwen, 34, market research

It can be difficult to fully imagine what life will be like after your baby's born, but one thing is certain—along with all the excitement will come a level of responsibility unlike anything you've known before. You may anticipate that most of it will fall on your shoulders and probably wonder if you'll ever be able to do anything else aside from care for your baby. Indulgences that have been a normal part of your life will soon have to be sacrificed. Time and money you've spent on yourself may for the first time have to be drastically curtailed. While you probably don't mind giving up certain things, you don't want to give up everything, and this can make you worry about how you're going to balance your needs with your baby's.

In her dream, Gwen is trying to figure out how she'll integrate taking care of herself with taking care of her baby. She gives birth while working out, symbolizing her hope that her baby won't get in the way of her lifestyle. This also describes her difficulty accepting the changes in her life that are about to occur. Up until now, Gwen has been able to focus on herself as much as she wants. One way she's done this is by staying in shape, and she's afraid after the baby's born, this part of her life will fall by the wayside and she might lose something that's been important to her and makes her feel good.

Gwen's having such a good time in her dream, enjoying her body and the attention she's getting, that she forgets what she did with her baby. When she panics, it expresses her fear that if she thinks about herself or her own needs in any way, her baby will somehow suffer as a result. In her dream, this fear is realized when she learns her husband has put their newborn in the vegetable drawer. His incompetence suggests that Gwen also worries she won't be able to depend upon anyone to share in the responsibility of caring for the baby, exacerbating her fear that soon she'll have no freedom at all.

Gwen's fear of losing her freedom is accompanied by guilt for wanting her freedom in the first place. In her dream, when she discovers her husband's put the baby in the refrigerator, it's like retribution for the time spent taking care of herself instead of the baby. If she hadn't desired the freedom to fulfill her own needs, she wouldn't have left the baby to begin with, and none of this would have happened.

Epilogue

While researching *Dreaming for Two,* we noticed a pattern. At first, most of the expectant mothers who participated in our book were hesitant to discuss their more complicated feelings and inner conflicts with us. But once they felt comfortable enough to begin talking, it was as if a veil had been lifted. They were able to express, often for the first time, that along with their joy in expecting a baby, they harbored darker, more confusing thoughts and feelings that are difficult to acknowledge. We also became aware of a troubling irony—these women, who shared so many of the same issues and feelings, felt alone with them, believing they were the only ones who had them.

We hope that *Dreaming for Two* has shown you that you're not alone with your feelings, and that one of the most important things you can do for yourself at this time is to connect with others who are experiencing feelings similar to your own. This can mean anything from finding or creating a support network of other mothers and mothers-to-be to simply reading this book and recognizing yourself within its pages. Connecting with others is a way of better understanding what you're going through and beginning to clear a path for yourself that will allow you to more fully enjoy your baby and yourself as a mother.

We also hope that during your expectant months, you will want to explore the myriad issues your dreams can reveal, and that you have been inspired to keep a dream journal of your own. This will help you figure out and appreciate what becoming a mother means to you, and years from now, you'll be able to remember this special time in your life not just through snapshots taken by loved ones and friends during your waking hours, but also through those nocturnal flights of fancy, your dreams.

About the Authors

Sindy Greenberg is a journalist who has written for *The New York Times, The New York Observer,* and *Gourmet,* among other publications. She lives in New York City.

Elyse Kroll is a senior editor at Martha Stewart Living Omnimedia. She lives with her husband and son in New York City.

Hillary Grill, M.S.W., is a psychotherapist in private practice. She has been on-staff at the Mount Sinai Medical Center. Her practice is in New York City, where she lives with her husband and two daughters.